BODY, SOUL & SPIRIT

GOD'S BUILDING BLOCKS

BODY, SOUL & SPIRIT

GOD'S BUILDING BLOCKS

DALE RUMBLE

Printed in the United States of America

Publishing services by Selah Publishing Group, LLC, Arizona. The views expressed or implied in this work do not necessarily reflect those of Selah Publishing Group.

ISBN 1-58930-086-6

Library of Congress Control Number: 2003092958

Acknowledgments & Dedication

I thank the Lord for the grace that He has given me to write, and I dedicate this book to all members of His body.

I thank my dear wife, Bertha, for her prayerful support, and for allowing me to take the time necessary to write.

I express my sincere thanks and grateful appreciation to Claudia Engel for her outstanding contribution in typing the manuscript, in designing the numerous graphics, as well as for her helpful suggestions concerning the text.

I would also like to thank Jessica Scott for her photographic work involved in the front cover, her creativity and expertise.

And lastly I extend thanks to two very good friends: James Garrett of Tulsa, Oklahoma, and Dr. John Hill of Victoria, British Columbia, who are men of great stature in handling the scriptures, for the time they devoted to reviewing the manuscript and for their insight and helpful criticisms.

CONTENTS

Introduction....................ix

Chapters Page#

1. The Creation of Man....................11
2. Our Faculties....................21
3. The Fall and Redemption of Man....................37
4. Education and Revelation....................63
5. Christian Character....................73
6. Our Priesthood....................97
7. Spiritual Warfare....................115
8. Christian Fellowship....................133
9. Ministry....................145
10. I Will Build My Church....................165

Appendix....................175

Introduction

To become a Christian is to begin a personal journey into that mysterious realm of the Spirit. This book has been written to provide a guide for this journey.

It has been said that a picture is worth a thousand words; I have found this to be true. Several years ago the Lord revealed to me a simple graphic image, a representation of body, soul and spirit, that made it much easier for me to understand spiritual truths and to teach others. This is what I wish to share with the reader.

Since God created man in His image, there is an important and necessary spiritual dimension to our being. We are made up of body, soul and spirit. Those three divine "building blocks" have been designed and woven together by God so that we may know Him, serve Him and become like Him. Our maturity in Christ, our relationship to Him and His people, and our sphere of service are intricately related to the role of the Holy Spirit in these three component parts of our being. The heart of understanding these things, and of yielding to the Spirit of God, requires that we distinguish and separate what is soulish from what is spiritual.

The scripture that is the basis for the graphics of this book is Hebrews 4:12, where God declares that His word is sharper than any two-edged sword to pierce and divide between soul and spirit. All information that we will ever receive in this life comes to us via one of two avenues; either through our five physical senses by which we relate to the world around us, or through spiritual senses which are our interface to the spirit world. These two avenues, or sources, are essentially windows into our soul. The graphic images in the text illustrate these two windows to visually distinguish between soul and spirit with a clarity that would be difficult to convey by words alone.

Psychology is the secular science of mind and behavior. Since this discipline does not recognize the redemptive influence of God's Spirit on the spirit of man, it is not pertinent, and therefore is not considered. When Christian counselors mix Bible truths with psychology the power of God's word is compromised. The goal of counseling is to produce a godly change in character of the counselee. The graphics in this book will clarify and make more understandable the Bible truths used by counselors to teach and confront others on behavior and personality.

Chapter 1

The Creation Of Man

A Picture is Worth a Thousand Words

I was often thwarted when I first began to teach the scriptures. The reason being an inability to explain the difference between the soul and the spirit. How does one describe something one can't see or touch? I knew the pertinent scriptures, so I would simply quote them in response to being questioned on the subject. However, something was lacking. It was apparent that those whom I taught also did not grasp the difference. They often confused their emotions with God's anointing. Frustrations arose because it was clear that the word of God, itself, should distinguish between these three parts of our being.

> *For the word of God is . . . sharper than any two-edged sword, . . . piercing as far as the division of soul and spirit. . . . (Hebrews 4:12)*

What was missing? It seemed as if I was wielding a dull sword. Even though I knew what the Bible had to say on the subject, my understanding fell short of what I knew the Lord desired, especially when I taught on subjects relating to the Holy Spirit. To make matters worse, upon requesting help from other teachers, I surprisingly found they had essentially little more understanding than I did. My next stop was the Christian book store—not one, but many. I searched for books written on the subject of "spirit, soul and body" and related themes. From these I accumulated a great deal of information, but very little satisfaction.

One day the Lord pointed out a simple truth to me: He had taught the people through the use of word pictures (visual aids). His sermons, rich with truth for the multitudes or His disciples, were couched in a language of imagery. Parables such as the *Sower and the Seed,* and our call to fruitfulness in the sermon on the *Vine and Branches* are some examples. Each truth was presented by giving the listeners a mental picture that vividly expressed the heart of what was being taught. In a sense, they were similar to flannel-graphs, picture slides and videos that are used to teach our children. A picture can be worth a thousand words!

This was part of the answer; the use of pictures would illustrate and explain the context of my thoughts. Since information is perceived through the senses, the Holy Spirit could then use both the visual and audio faculties of the audiences to bring a greater understanding. But one question remained, what picture would say what I meant? What construct could be used to represent the sprit, soul and body? In the literature researched, the only model I had discovered was one of three concentric circles, where the innermost circle denoted the spirit and the outer circle denoted the body. This contributed little to my understanding, so it was discarded and I asked the Lord to show me a simpler model that would be more effective. The answer to that prayer is what I share with you now in this book.

We are Fearfully and Wonderfully Made

It is not uncommon to find Christians who view themselves as a duality; that is, as having two parts to their beings. This mind-set arises out of the concept of "an inner (spiritual) man" and "an outer (physical) man." It is true there are two worlds—the spiritual and the physical; it is also true that in our inclination toward the things of God, the scriptures speak of us as being either "spiritually minded" or "fleshly minded" (Romans 8:5-8; 1 Corinthians 3:1). However, these two conflicting natures do *not* mean there are only two parts to our personhood.

We are, of course, made up of spirit, soul and body. Indeed, it is only as we properly understand each dimension of our beings that we can fully appropriate those spiritual provisions which are ours in Christ. To this end, the word of God is important, for as the sword of the Spirit, it will divide soul from spirit.

One of the first lessons we learn is that the Lord is interested in our total being: body, soul and spirit. Each part is to reflect the fruit of our salvation. All we are and all we do should glorify Him.

> *Now may the God of peace Himself sanctify you* ***entirely;*** *and may your* ***spirit and soul and body*** *be preserved* ***complete, without blame*** *at the coming of our Lord Jesus Christ. (1 Thessalonians 5:23)*

The righteousness of Jesus is to become visible in our *whole* person. This is what He died for and what He expects to find in us when He returns. How do we prepare ourselves? How do we develop all components of our being without neglecting one part? What balance do we pursue between physical exercise, education and spiritual training? To begin with, consider the first recorded words of God concerning man's creation:

> *. . . let us make man* ***in Our image,*** *according to* ***Our likeness*** *. . . . (Genesis 1:26)*

John 4:24 makes it clear that God is spirit. For this reason, our likeness to Him must be spiritual.

The act of creation involved two distinct steps (see Figure 1). The first step concerns our bodies.

> *Then the Lord God formed man of dust from the ground. (Genesis 2:7)*

After stating His intention of making man in His likeness and for the purpose of ruling the earth, the Lord God took dust from the earth, over which Adam was to have dominion. From this He fashioned a physical body, which is depicted as the bottom circle of our diagram. This action expressed the following thought: "If you are going to rule over the earth, you must be a part of it; you must be intimately identified with it."

In summary, the first step of creation prepared a body (or clay vessel) for Adam to dwell in. Our bodies are earthly tents which we will inhabit as long as we live in this world, or until Jesus returns.

The next creative step involved spirit and life.

> *. . . and (the Lord God) breathed into his nostrils the* ***breath*** *of life; and man became a* ***living soul.*** *(Genesis 2:7)*

In this second step, God breathed life from the essence of His own being into the clay body. He did more than speak a creative word—He gave of Himself in the act!

We recognize that the Spirit of God is not air. Consequently, what happened was more than placing oxygen into Adam's lungs. God is spirit, and He breathed the properties of His life and nature into the vessel of

"LET US MAKE MAN IN OUR IMAGE ACCORDING TO OUR LIKENESS"

GENESIS 1:26-27; 2:7

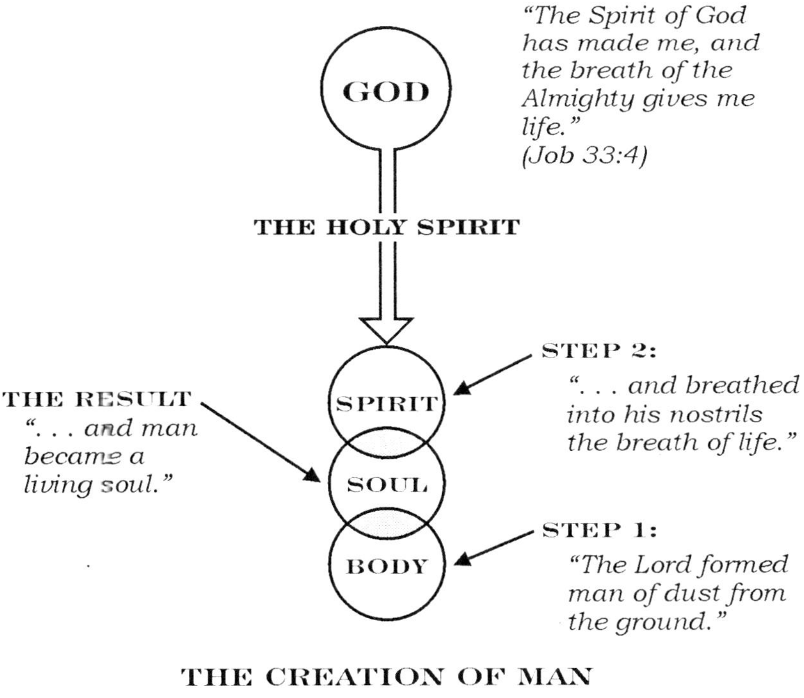

THE CREATION OF MAN

FIGURE 1

clay. If Adam was to represent the Lord in ruling the earth, he must partake of the Lord's nature. The breath of God was the Holy Spirit, who brought both spiritual and physical life into Adam. God did not breathe into any of the animals He had created since they only received natural life at their creation. Nor did He breathe into the woman, for she was taken out of Adam who already possessed the life of God These words of Job sum up this creative step:

> *The **Spirit** of God made me, and the **breath** of the Almighty gives me life. (Job 33:4)*

The spiritual life imparted to Adam is depicted by the circle labeled "spirit" (Figure 1). He possessed physical life because of the air he breathed. This life was sustained from the physical environment he ruled over. However, his spiritual life came from the union he had with God in the Holy Spirit. This "spirit-life" is the source of all that is required to make man into God's likeness. Only by it could Adam fulfill the commission given to him. As long as the Holy Spirit remained in the spirit of Adam, he was immortal, being sustained by life from above. The supernatural qualities of divine life from the Spirit of God mingled with the physical properties of the earth were blended together in the creation of a new being. Man became a *"living soul"*; he was a soul, he had a spirit and he had a body. He was a living soul because of the life properties of his spirit.

Adam was commissioned to rule over the earth for the Lord. To this end he was made from *both* the substance of God and the substance of the earth. He was intimately identified with both realms. This dual set of properties will be with all who have been born of the Spirit until the Lord Jesus returns and they receive new, immortal bodies like His own.

W.E. Vine's *An Expository Dictionary of New Testament Words* defines the constituent parts of man as follows:

> The spirit may be recognized as the life principle bestowed on man by God, the soul as the resulting life constituted in the individual, the body being the material organism animated by soul and spirit (p. 54, Vol. IV).

Vine further states that "spirit and soul can be distinguished but not separated in fact." In other words, a human soul without a spirit has no meaning. Whether on earth, in hell, or in the presence of God, one's soul and spirit are always united. Together they are, in fact, what comprises a person; the body is merely a vehicle or house in which they dwell. The soul-spirit combination is an immortal being; it will always exist.

The two words used in scripture to define spirit, Hebrew *(Ruach)* and Greek *(Pneuma)*, are also used at times to mean "breath." Air (or oxygen) is the basis of body (or physical) life, just as spirit is the basis of soul life. Oxygen is made available to the various parts of our bodies through the blood stream. Thus, the life of the flesh is in the blood because of the oxygen we breathe.

> *For the life of the flesh is in the blood, and I have given it to you on the altar to make atonement for your souls; for it is the blood by reason of the life that makes atonement. (Leviticus 17:11)*

We will never "lose" our spirits, but we do lose our breath when we physically die. We are mortal in a physiological (or body) sense of the word. We will always exist in a psychological (or soul) sense because of our spirit. However, we *live* spiritually *only* if our spirit contains the Spirit of God. This is what constitutes eternal life; separation from God is the ultimate and most awful form of death. Spiritual death is a state of existence by a conscious being who is separated from the life of God.

Figure 2 illustrates the mortal and immortal aspects of our being. That we are a soul is substantiated by numerous scriptures. A sinner's salvation is always referred to as the salvation of his soul. He has become alive in his spirit; as a being, he is a redeemed soul.

> *For what will a man be profited, if he gains the whole world, and forfeits his soul? Or what shall a man give in exchange for his soul? (Matthew 16:26)*

> *. . . but now you have returned to the Shepherd and Guardian of your souls. (1 Peter 2:5)*

> *. . . he who turns a sinner from the error of his way will save his soul from death . . . (James 5:20)*

> *. . . the first man Adam, became a living soul . . . (1 Corinthians 15:45)*

> *. . . but we are . . . of those who have faith to the preserving of the soul. (Hebrews 10:39)*

We are indeed fearfully and wonderfully made. God foreknew us, spirit, soul and body while we were still in our mother's womb. He made us so that we can embrace His purpose and glorify Him. We have been made

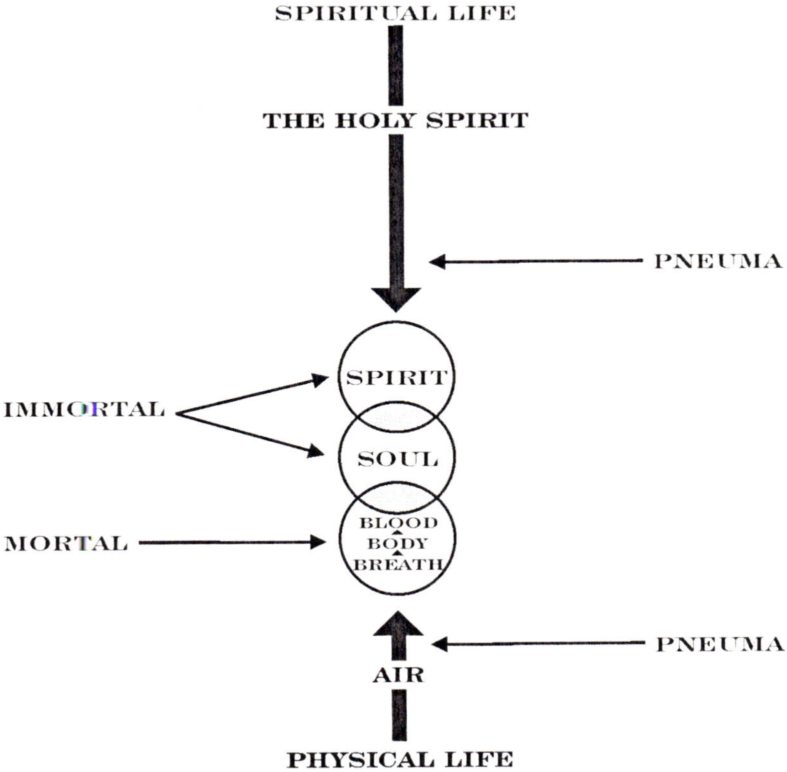

LIFE

FIGURE 2

for Him and nothing less will satisfy the deep longing within us, a longing inherent in our spirit.

Having defined the three primary constituent parts of our person, let us next briefly examine the role of our faculties which are anointed by the Holy Spirit to bring us into a deep, personal relationship with our Creator. This process is more than acquiring mental concepts or hidden knowledge. It is achieving an experiential reality of intimately knowing the Lord Jesus Christ as Savior, Lord and Friend. How does the Holy Spirit accomplish this wonderful work?

In succeeding chapters the graphic model of body, soul and spirit, in concert with text, addresses pertinent subjects such as: how God communicates with man, waging spiritual warfare, the spirit of revelation, putting on the image of God, grace versus law, spiritual gifts and ministries, etc.

We will discover that the One who created and redeemed us is the most important Person and emphasis in our life and ministry! He is the center and source of all truth.

Chapter 2

Our Faculties

Windows of the Soul

Many people like to live along the seashore. Imagine for a moment that your home overlooks the sea on one side, and on the other side it commands a view of a well-landscaped garden with shrubs and flowers. If the house was designed with two picture windows, one looking out to sea and the other overlooking the land, there would be a choice of two views.

It is very much the same in our souls. We live in an earthen house, which is our body. We experience two realms of influence, for we are related to two worlds. Like the house, we have two windows. Through these windows come all the information that we receive.

These windows are illustrated in Figure 3. They are the two areas created where the soul circle overlaps the body and the spirit circles respectively. All sensor and intuitive inputs to the soul must come through these two windows. The two overlapping areas are shown in this way since they represent faculties, that in one case, have attributes of both soul and body, and in the other instance, attributes of soul and spirit. All information received into one's mind is perceived either through spiritual or physical senses, which are what these two areas represent. I have chosen to call them windows since they pass information into the mind, much like real windows allow one to view a landscape. Just as one window in our imaginary house portrays the garden, while the other presents a view of the sea, so physical senses receive stimuli from the

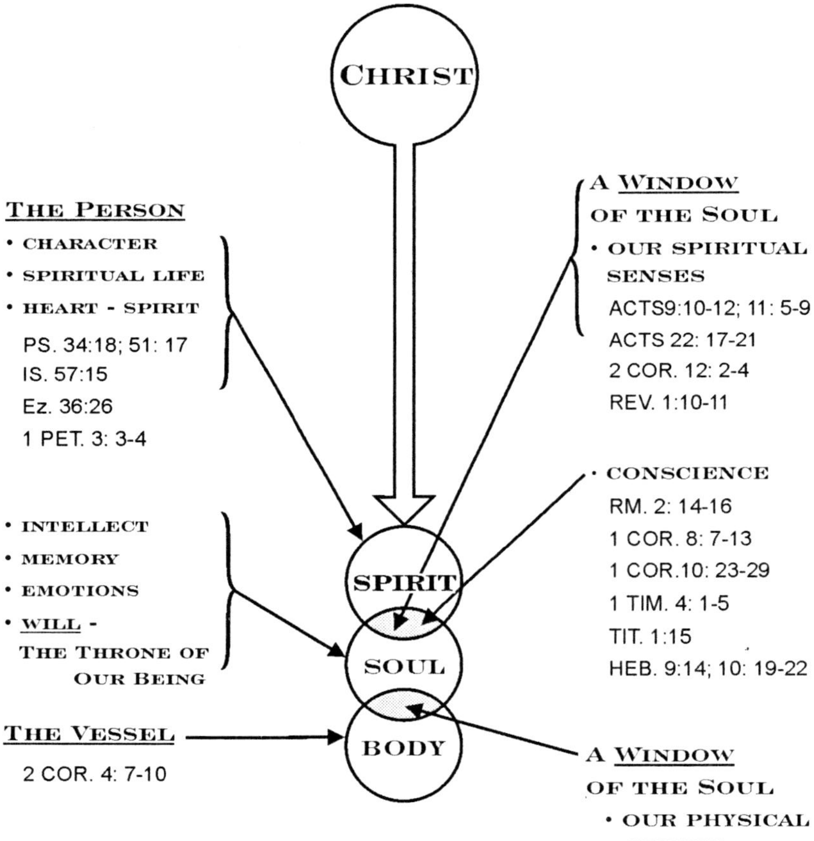

OUR FACULTIES

FIGURE 3

physical world, and spiritual senses provide intuitive input from the spirit world. Thus, these two interfaces to sensory inputs are windows of the soul.

Let us consider our five natural senses. It is apparent these sense organs are flesh and blood, and therefore they clearly are part of the body. However, the invisible impulses of the senses which flow from them through nerves and impress their messages into our minds, do not have physical dimensions, and consequently they are part of the soul. Thus, the lower of the two overlapped areas represents a window of natural senses. Through it, we experience the senses of touch, taste, sight, sound and smell. It is a window facing out to the physical world around us. Through it come temptations that could draw us away from God if we yielded to them. However, it is also the window through which we receive the gospel by sight and sound. Clearly we must know how to discipline the use of this window. Our senses are to serve us; they must not become our master.

The spirit world around us cannot be experienced through natural senses. Some who are unfamiliar with the spirit world may speak of a "sixth sense" of intuition when referring to knowledge that is mysteriously outside the realm of their five senses. Ignorance and curiosity have led many into deception and destruction as they explored this spirit world through occult practices. There is a wonderful world of light and life to be experienced through the Spirit of God. However, there is also a terrible world of spiritual darkness seeking to capture and enslave the spirits of lost men; this must be avoided at all costs.

The realm of intuition involves spiritual senses. These are shown in the model of Figure 3 as the upper, overlapped area of spirit and soul. When a human spirit is indwelt by the Holy Spirit, that person "becomes alive" in Christ, and his "inner man" can receive anointings of insight from the Lord through this window.

Education is acquired through physical senses, but spiritual knowledge is received by revelation. There are biblical records of Christians who have been caught up in the Spirit to hear and see things that could not be received through their natural senses. The Bible states that no man can look upon God and live. His glory would blind us or even consume us (Acts 9:3-8; 1 Timothy 6:16). However, through the anointing of the Holy Spirit He can be seen, as evidenced by John's experience in the Book of Revelation. The following are some biblical examples of spiritual senses:

> *I was in the city of Joppa praying; and in a trance I* ***saw*** *a vision, an object coming down like a great sheet lowered by four corners from the sky; and it came right down to me, and when I had* ***fixed my gaze*** *upon it and* ***was observing*** *it, I saw the four-footed animals of the earth and the wild beasts and the crawling creatures and the birds of the air. And I also* ***heard*** *a voice* ***saying*** *to me, "Get up, Peter; kill and eat." But I said, "By no means, Lord . . . . (Acts 11:5-8)*

In this particular experience, Peter reports himself as "seeing," "hearing" and speaking"; however, he was *not* using natural faculties or senses. The Lord anointed Peter's spiritual senses and communicated with him while he was in a trance.

The following is a similar example in the life of Paul:

> *A vision **appeared** to Paul in the night: A certain man of Macedonia was standing and appealing to him, and **saying**, "come over to Macedonia and help us." (Acts 16:9)*

The reality of communication in the Spirit is just as valid as what one would experience by physical senses. It may not be as common, but it is no less real. Paul describes one such experience which was so vivid he did not know whether he had been physically caught up to Paradise or was in the Spirit.

> *I know a man in Christ who fourteen years ago—whether in the body I do not know, or out of the body I do not know, God knows—such a man was caught up to the third heaven. And I know how such a man—whether in the body or apart from the body I do not know, God knows—was caught up into Paradise, and **heard** inexpressible words, which a man is not permitted to speak. (2 Corinthians 12:2-4)*

The Book of Revelation was given to John by the Spirit. As we see from the record of his words, it involved his spiritual senses:

> *I was **in the Spirit** on the Lord's day, and I **heard** behind me a loud voice like the sound of a trumpet, saying, "Write in a book what you **see** . . . (Revelation 1:10-11)*

The dialogue, messages and symbolic visions that followed were all given to him through the Spirit. His natural senses were not at play as he was instructed on what to write. The revelation that John recorded came to him directly from heaven.

One of many examples of the use of spiritual senses in the ministry of the Lord Jesus was His vision of Nathaniel under the fig tree (John 1:47-50).

Conscience

In the soul-spirit window of spiritual senses there is another important faculty called "conscience." Our conscience is a bridle of the Lord for it is where the Spirit of God guides us by imparting an inner knowing that something is, or is not, correct. It does *not* depend on one's foreknowledge; it is simply intuitive knowledge from the Holy Spirit. Because it involves impressions of the Spirit on one's mind, conscience is part of both soul and spirit. It is important to heed what we perceive in our consciences from the Lord. If we consistently act contrary to it, we can over time, become hard or seared in our conscience and lose sensitivity to His voice.

The function of conscience is made clear by the following scripture:

> *For when Gentiles who do not have the Law do* ***instinctively*** *the things of the Law, these, not having the Law, are a law to themselves, in that they show the work of the Law written in their hearts,* ***their conscience bearing*** *witness, and their thoughts alternately accusing or else defending them . . . (Romans 2:14-15)*

Paul's rejection of the Holy Spirit's impressions upon his conscience prior to conversion are described by God as "kicking against a sharp object."

> *And . . . I heard a voice saying to me in the Hebrew dialect, "Saul, Saul, why are persecuting*

> *Me? It is hard for you to kick against the goads. (Acts 26:14)*

A believer's conscience is to bear witness to the mind of the Spirit (Romans 9:1). For this reason, our conscience should always be pure and tender. However, one's conscience can also be affected by the teaching of men. Depending upon what is taught, this can be good or bad. For example, when children are properly taught to avoid sin, their consciences are conditioned to turn away from evil. This is good. However, teaching that certain traditions or doctrines are from God when, in fact they are not, brings people into bondage. Legalism is an example of this.

Attempting to please God by a righteousness based on keeping laws has always been a great hindrance to His people.

Believers who accept such bondage become "weak in faith" for their conscience has been defiled.

> ***All** things (pertaining to food and drink) are lawful, but **not all things are profitable. All** things are lawful, but **not all things edify**. Let no one seek his own good, but that of his neighbor. Eat **anything** that is sold in the meat market, without asking questions **for conscience' sake**; for the earth is the Lord's, and all it contains. If one of the unbelievers invites you, and you wish to go, eat **anything** that is set before you, without asking questions **for conscience' sake.** But if anyone should say to you, "This is meat sacrificed to idols," do not eat it, **for the sake of the one who informed you, and for conscience' sake;** I mean **not your own conscience, but the other man's;** for why is my freedom judged by another's con-*

> *science? . . . Whether, then, you eat or drink or whatever you do, do all to the glory of God.* ***Give no offense either to Jews or to Greeks or to the church of God.*** *(1 Corinthians 10:23-32)*

How are we to relate to believers who are weak in faith? While we are to remain free in our own conscience, we must never act in our freedom so as to offend the conscience of others.

> *Therefore let us not judge one another any more, but rather determine this—**not to put an obstacle or a stumbling block in another's way.** I know and am convinced in the Lord Jesus that nothing is unclean in itself; but to him who thinks anything to be unclean, to him it is unclean For if because of food your brother is hurt, you are no longer walking according to love. Do not destroy with your food him for whom Christ died . . . **for the kingdom of God is not eating and drinking, but righteousness and peace and joy in the Holy Spirit** . . . do not tear down the work of God for the sake of food. All things indeed are clean, but they are evil for the man who eats and gives offense. It is good not to eat meat or to drink wine, or to do anything by which your brother stumbles (Romans 14:13-15, 17, 20-21).*

> ***But take care lest this liberty of yours somehow become a stumbling block to the weak.*** *For if someone sees you who have knowledge dining in an idol's temple, will not his conscience, if he is weak, be strengthened to eat things sacrificed to idols? For through your knowledge he who is weak is ruined, the brother for whose sake Christ*

> *died, And so, by sinning against the brethren and* ***wounding their conscience when it is weak,*** *you sin against Christ. (1 Corinthians 8: 9-12)*

It is wrong to encourage those weak in the faith to act against (or violate) their consciences. However, it is proper to give them remedial instruction if they will hear you, for there is no virtue in ignorance!

The way of righteousness is to walk under the law of the Spirit of life in Christ Jesus (Romans 8:2). This transcends all other law. It is the *perfect* law, for it is the law of liberty. Wherever the Spirit is Lord, there is *liberty to choose* His way of life (2 Corinthians 3:17). It is the way of *choice*, and not the way of compulsion. The righteousness that God seeks to bring forth in our lives *can* only come out of our freedom to choose to be led by the Holy Spirit.

Recognizing this truth helps us to guard against legalism, false teaching and the doctrine of demons, all of which corrupt the consciences of men.

> *But the Spirit explicitly says that in later times some will fall away from the faith, paying attention to deceitful spirits and doctrines of demons, by means of the* ***hypocrisy of liars seared in their own conscience*** *as with a branding iron, men who forbid marriage and advocate abstaining from foods . . . . (1 Timothy 4: 1-3)*

A pure spirit will be marked by a pure conscience.

> *To the pure, all things are pure; but to those who are defiled and unbelieving, nothing is pure, but both their mind and their conscience are defiled. (Titus 1: 15)*

Great care must be exercised to ensure that the consciences of those being trained and discipled are kept pure and tender for the Lord's guidance. It is the rein of our harness in the Spirit.

Will the Real Person Please Stand Up!

What we see when we look at one another is not the real person. Our bodies grow old, change with time and eventually die. In the resurrection we will appear quite different from what we are in this life. The real person lives on the inside and is known by various manifestations of life that are distinct and separate from the physical body. Some life expressions are: character, reasoning, will, intelligence, memory, emotions and mental attitude. These properties define what we really are.

All of these, except for character, relate to the soul realm of a person. The will defines the capability to make decisions, and as such, is the place of government in our lives. It is the throne of our beings. Without a personal will we would only be robots. As we submit our wills to leadings of the Holy Spirit, coming to us through our soul-spirit window, then Jesus becomes our Lord in fact.

When Jesus walked on earth, His will was submitted to His Father at all times. The suffering of His soul during His passion is clear in the following scripture:

> *Then He said to them, "My soul is deeply grieved, to the point of death; remain here and keep watch with Me. (Matthew 26: 38)*

> *As a result of the anguish of His soul, He will see it and be satisfied . . . . (Isaiah 53: 11)*

Jesus did not hang on the cross until He expired. When all scripture was fulfilled concerning His ministry on earth as our Savior, He dismissed His spirit. This act illustrates the primacy of His will.

> *When Jesus therefore had received the sour wine, He said, "It is finished!" And He bowed His head, and gave up His spirit. (John 19: 30)*

In summary, we receive information into our souls from two windows, one from the physical world and one from the spirit world. Through the exercise of our wills, we control which realm we are guided by; we choose which window we will spend most of our time at. According to our choice and self-discipline (or lack of it), over time, we will take on the characteristics of one of these worlds. The Lord calls to us through the spirit-soul window, for this is the window by which we can become like Him. The choice is ours.

Emotions

Emotions are affective responses of feeling from one's consciousness in response to input from the senses. They are affective since they condition how one may act in response to such input. Some obvious emotions are: happiness, fear, anger, shame, frustration, etc. Together with behavioral traits they express an individual's personality. As such they are located in the soul circle of our model.

We are familiar with the role of our emotions in response to our physical senses in every day life. However, the Holy Spirit can also touch the consciousness of believers through their spiritual senses. This may take place when the Holy Spirit anoints one for visions (including dreams), revelation or for one of the spiritual gifts. The response in emotions could include: joy, peace, boldness, thankfulness, etc. Should the Lord desire to do so, He can touch believers in such a way that their response would be much more demonstrative, such as joyful laughter, deep weeping, being "slain" or "drunk" in the Spirit, etc.

Satan seeks to draw men, women and children after him through their emotional response to the sensory appeal of drugs, alcohol, pornography, witchcraft, violence, etc.

Believers must control what they allow to come through the window of their physical senses. Nothing is as important as our union with Christ in the Holy Spirit. It is out of the simplicity of our souls and the purity of our hearts that we will grow in knowledge of Him.

To grow in God, we must know our hearts and learn to judge our motives. Unless we understand such things about ourselves, we will not know how to counsel and train others. The secret is spending time in His presence, studying His word so that it becomes a mirror in which we see ourselves. It will differentiate between soul and spirit and remove any confusion that may exist concerning these areas of our being.

> *For the word of God is living and active and sharper than any two-edged sword, and* ***piercing as far as the division of soul and spirit,*** *of both joints and marrow, and able to judge the thoughts and intentions of the heart. (Hebrews 4:12)*

Dreams and Visions

Visions can occur while one is conscious or in a trance. Dreams are mental activities that take place just below the threshold of consciousness. God uses dreams to speak to His people, often as warnings (Job 33:14-18; Matthew 2:12, 19, 22). The Holy Spirit impresses dreams in the form of thoughts or visions on their spiritual senses while people are asleep. Emotions may be involved. Dreams are often symbolic so that they need interpretation. However, dreams can also be clear messages.

While a young Christian, I was part of a local church where division had broken out that was marked by much ungodly gossip and criticism. During this time, I had a dream in which I found myself in a bathroom that was very dirty with used tissues and paper towels covering the floor. I felt a compulsion to pick up tissues and put them in my mouth. I awoke with a feeling of revulsion, and immediately knew that the Lord was warning me not to take part in the gossip and criticism.

Dreams and visions should not be uncommon. The great outpouring of the Holy spirit that gave birth to the church was marked by dreams and visions as well as miracles and prophecies (Acts 2:14-17).

Heart-Spirit

The Lord frequently points out the importance of the human spirit by referring to it as "heart" in some scriptures. The reason He did so is because man has always understood the supreme importance of his heart in physical life. If it is diseased, life expectancy is shortened; when it stops, death is the result. Our physical health, therefore, is very much a question of how healthy our heart is.

When speaking of spiritual life the same dependent relationship exists with one's spirit. Here, character is developed; it is the place where the Holy Spirit abides within us. A proud, haughty, hard spirit implies a sick spiritual life. The same is true for an unruly or deceitful spirit. Such heart attitudes will limit the Holy Spirit's anointing to one's spiritual senses. On the other hand, *a humble, contrite spirit denotes spiritual health*. The Lord reveals Himself and teaches His ways to those who are humble of heart. The importance of our heart attitude *cannot* be overemphasized. We are commanded to be diligent and watch over the state of our spirit, for from it flow springs of life (Proverbs 4:23). The following verses are examples where "heart" is used as a synonym of "spirit."

> *The Lord is near to the* ***brokenhearted*** *and saves those who are* ***crushed in spirit****. (Psalm 34: 18)*

> *The sacrifices of God are a* ***broken spirit;*** *a broken and a* ***contrite heart****, O God, Thou wilt not despise. (Psalm 51: 17)*

> *I dwell on a high and holy place, and also with the* ***contrite and lowly of spirit*** *in order to revive the* ***spirit of the lowly*** *and to* ***revive the heart of the contrite.*** *(Isaiah 57: 15)*

> *. . . But let it be the* ***hidden person of the heart,*** *with the imperishable quality of a* ***gentle and quiet*** *spirit, which is precious in the sight of God. (1 Peter 3: 4)*

. . . So that Christ may dwell in your hearts through faith. (Ephesians 3:17)

The word is near you, in your mouth and in your heart . . . if you . . . believe in your heart . . . for with the heart a person believes, resulting in righteousness . . . . (Romans 10: 8-10)

Certainly Christ does not live in physical hearts, neither is there any faculty to believe there. The word "heart" in the above scriptures refers to one's spirit. This is where Christ dwells; it is here He touches our conscience and brings us spiritual understanding of His word. Here character is developed; this is where we become like Him.

Natural life is sustained from the air we breathe because our bodies require oxygen to live. Similarly we live spiritually *only* if the Holy Spirit abides within our spirits. He is "spiritual oxygen," if you will. The basic disciplines for physical health are to breathe, eat and exercise properly. The corresponding disciplines for a sound spiritual life are to be filled with the Holy Spirit, eat the word of God and walk in the law of the Spirit of life in Christ Jesus.

We must also care for our bodies as well as our spirits, for they are temples of the Holy Spirit. We have a stewardship entrusted to us for our *total* being. An unhealthy body, or bad physical habits can hinder spiritual growth; but even more important, an unhealthy spirit or mind can destroy one's body. Perhaps the best example of the latter is the destructive results of harboring hatred and unforgiveness. Food, diet and exercise must play a part in the discipline of our lives if we are to glorify the Lord in our total being. One who is greatly overweight will find it difficult to disciple others on the virtue of moderation. Poor nutrition, inadequate exercise or rest, excessive stress, pollution in the air we breathe, the food we eat, or in the water we drink can all trigger or aggravate psychological problems in individuals. Thus, although our hearts are most important, we are to take care of ourselves as a whole and complete being: body, soul and spirit.

Mind

In scripture the word "mind" refers to more than the faculty of thought. It is used to express a person's disposition toward righteousness. One's perception, feelings, thoughts, intentions and desires as willfully expressed in word and deed come from either a fleshly (carnal) or a spiritual mind.

> *For those who are according to the flesh set their minds on the things of the flesh, but those who are according to the Spirit, the things of the Spirit. For the mind set on the flesh is death, but the mind set on the Spirit is life and peace. (Romans 8:5-6)*

Because of our fallen nature, it is very important to seek for renewal of our mind; a subject that will be addressed in the following chapter.

Chapter 3

The Fall and Redemption of Man

The First Sin

Did Adam experience an inner conflict between right and wrong when he was first created? The answer is no, for he was fully united with God and had no knowledge of evil. He existed in a state of innocence. He was one with his Creator; they were united in spirit. That is, until sin entered the picture.

Adam was not created to function as a robot. He possessed the capability to make decisions. In his soul were the faculties of intellect, emotions, memory, and above all *will*, the center of decision making. Adam was free to do as he pleased. He could choose to go his own way or to obey God. The Lord requires that we serve Him through the exercise of a free will, a faculty which is essentially the throne of our being. As long as Adam walked in harmony and obedience to his Lord he had no inner conflict with evil.

The Lord had created woman as a helper, or helpmate, to complete Adam so they could multiply and fill the earth. She was made from a rib taken from around Adam's heart, being literally made from his substance. God did not breathe life into her, for she partook of the life already present in Adam. The will of God was made known to Adam, and through him to his wife. In their creation God made them both in His likeness, each having a free will. They were commissioned together in a relationship patterned after that existing between Adam and the Lord: unity with headship. They were to live as one; what they did was to reflect the harmony of God's will. As long as they were united in purpose to obey the Lord, His life remained within them and they were immortal. In this way, they could rule and subdue the earth, for they possessed the mind and power of God. They were literally an extension of His life on the earth. The choice to obey or not to obey was theirs.

How they fell into sin reveals the shrewd and cunning nature of our adversary. The first step Satan undertook in his deception was to break the bond of headship between Adam and his wife. He tempted the woman to make a decision relating to God's specific command independent of her husband. When she consented to debate and reason with him without consulting Adam, the first step toward sin had been taken. Rebellion against authority was the sin that Lucifer himself had committed in the beginning (Isaiah 14:12-14). Having succeeded in this, Satan next persuaded her to disobey the Lord and eat from the tree of "the knowledge of good and evil." His temptation was an appeal to her senses of sight and taste. He also appealed to her ego and intellect by promising her that she would be like God, knowing good and evil. Any doctrine which promises a short cut in becoming like God, is pure deception.

It is important to note that she was tempted in her soul, where reason, emotions, senses and will were involved. She was tempted to act from stimuli to her senses instead of obeying the Spirit of God. Consequently, she was deceived. Although Adam also sinned, he did so knowing what he was doing and was not deceived (1 Timothy 2:14). In either case, with sin came death and spiritual separation from God.

Satan's temptation of the woman is typical of how he attempts to deceive us. The thrusts of his temptation were the same desires that caused him to fall:

1. He rejected the headship that was upon his life (Isaiah 14:13).

2. He sought to be like God (Isaiah 14:14).

3. He was tempted in the realm of his spiritual senses (Ezekiel 28:17).

These were also the avenues of appeal he unsuccessfully tempted the Lord Jesus with:

1. Rise up and "exercise your authority" (Matthew 4:6).

2. Be like God "the easy way" (Matthew 4:8-9).

3. Sense of hunger (Matthew 4:3).

The essence of Satan's temptations is the promotion of self!

Consequences of the Fall

When Adam sinned, he abdicated his place under God as lord of the earth, and opened himself to the influences of Satan. As a result, Satan became ruler, or prince, of the earth and its atmospheric heaven (John 14:30). He has placed fallen angels as centers of authority in the heavens over lawlessness in cities, nations and men.

The earth, not willingly, but because of Adam's sin, came under the influence of Satan. Until now it groans and suffers under this curse, awaiting the day of release and deliverance when Satan's hold will be broken. When one comes to Christ, through faith with repentance, and receives Him as Lord and Savior, that person is delivered from the authority of Satan and is brought into the Kingdom of God.

The unsaved in the world live under the deception of the ruler of darkness and his cohorts. There are four reasons why men are in darkness:

1. They love and prefer darkness (John 3:19).

2. They are ignorant of the ways of God (Ephesians 4:17-18).

3. They are deceived (Matthew 6:22-23).

4. Their heart attitude toward others is one of hatred.

> *. . . The one who hates his brother is in darkness and walks in the darkness . . . . (1 John 2:11)*

One or more of these properties mark the hearts of lost mankind. The gospel is the answer for all of them, although not all who hear will respond. For example, there is very little hope for those who love darkness, while there is hope for the ignorant.

Life and Death

We are eternal beings; that is, we will always exist in a spirit-soul sense. However, we live spiritually only if we possess the Spirit of life. Adam died spiritually when he fell as a result of sin. He lost his union with God when the Holy Spirit left him. As Adam's descendants, each one of us have inherited this state of spiritual death in the fallen nature passed down to us. Thus, even though we may be alive physically, we are dead spiritually until life has been reestablished through the Holy Spirit coming to abide in our spirits. This renewal of life is spoken of as the "new birth."

If one dies physically without having received spiritual life, he is eternally separated from God in what is called the second death. Thus, if we are only born once, we must die twice; but if we have been born twice (physical and spiritual) we need only die once. Physical death for a Christian merely means leaving the body and going into the presence of the Lord (2 Corinthians 5:1-6).

The essence of true life, therefore, lies in the spiritual bond between our spirit (or heart) and the Lord. We have been made alive together with Christ. His Spirit will guide us in all matters of life and conduct. He who joins himself to the Lord is one spirit with Him (1 Corinthians 6:17). Through this union we have the potential for the character of God to be built into our hearts, and to have the mind of Christ to guide us.

The fall and the redemption of man is illustrated in Figures 4 and 5. It is important to recognize how God's provision for our redemption reflects His heart of love. His deep, unfathomable love for us is the reason for the cross of Christ; love is the basis of our redemption.

Repentance

Repentance is an *absolutely* necessary step in redemption for it involves an act of the will without which one could not be saved. True repentance includes the honesty to confess and acknowledge one's sin and

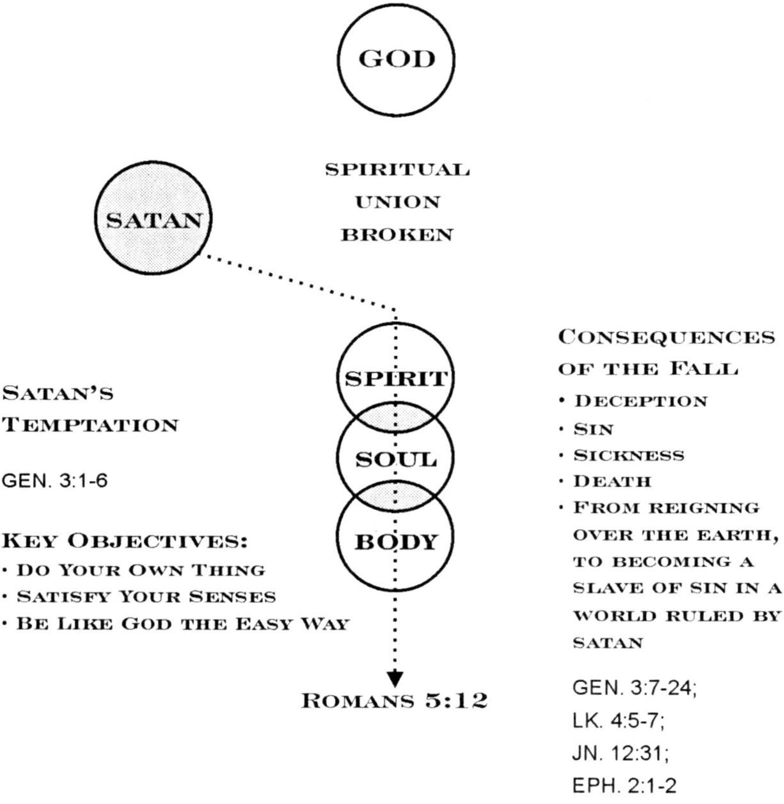

THE FALL OF MAN

FIGURE 4

THE CROSS

1 COR. 1:18-29
1 PET. 2:24
GAL. 6:14

REPENTANCE

2 CHRON. 7:13-14
2 PET. 3:9
RM. 2:4

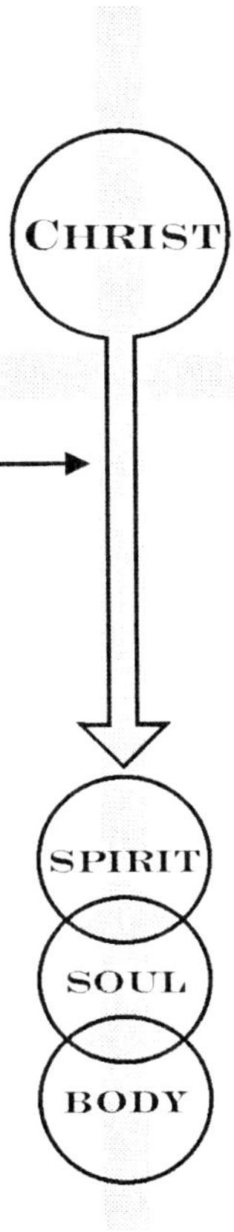

THE HOLY SPIRIT →

JN. 3:3-8
JN. 14:16-17, 26
JN. 16:7-15
TIT. 3:4-7

FAITH

RM. 5: 1-2
RM. 10:6-17
GAL. 2:16-20
GAL. 3:1-26
HEB. 11

RIGHTEOUSNESS

RM. 1:16-17
RM. 3:21-26
RM. 5:17-21
1 COR. 1:30
2 COR. 5:21

RENEWAL OF OUR MIND

IS. 55:8-9
RM. 12:1-3
EPH. 4:22-24
MT. 11:28-30
2 COR. 10:3-6

THE REDEMPTION OF MAN

FIGURE 5

disobedience before God and men. Equally important, it means *being willing to forsake* the ways of sin, and with God's help, to walk in righteousness. Sorrow for the past *alone* is not repentance; there must be an exercise of one's will to *forsake* habit patterns of sin and to *embrace* the way of truth.

Repentance is the first step to be taken when a Christian discovers he has fallen short of the will of God. We need to be quick to repent. Whenever this is found to be difficult, it is a sign that one's heart is becoming cold. This is a very dangerous position to be in; immediately, everything else should be laid aside and the Lord sought in humility. The Lord is near the brokenhearted; and He extends grace to the humble.

It is interesting to note that John the Baptist, Jesus, and Peter prefaced their proclamation of the gospel by the need to repent (Matthew 3:1-2; 4:17; Acts 2:38).

In the process of training leaders, making disciples and equipping saints, the supreme importance of *"instant repentance"* must be stamped into hearts. Far too often the place for repentance is masked by man-made laws; legalism becomes the measuring rod for righteousness and the heart is ignored. True repentance requires a yielded will and a contrite heart; and the *only* men God can use to extend His kingdom are broken men.

Whereas there are many kinds and classes of men in the world, the cross normalizes all who come to Christ. There are no great, small, wise, mighty or debased at Calvary. All men become sinners saved by grace, and each one is a potential candidate for the character and mind of Christ. When training disciples, *everything* must be referenced to the cross. Many bring their human values and talents into the kingdom, and these must be dealt with by the cross. Only what arises from their death can be used by God (1 Corinthians 1:18-31).

The Holy Spirit in Redemption

There is no redemption apart from the work of the Holy Spirit. It is He who reproves, convicts of sin and draws men to God. He reveals the dimensions of God's love as demonstrated in the substitutionary death of His Son. He magnifies the sacrifice of Jesus, the perfect lamb of God, who freely gave himself for all who were lost in sin. He brings the grace and power of His indwelling presence to those who respond in faith. He exalts the Lord Jesus, unveiling His glory and ways to those who are saved; and His promptings become the law of the Spirit of life to those who will walk in them. He reveals the heart of God to His people. Out of His revelations we find our call and place in the body of Christ, and understand how to embrace God's purpose for our lives.

We have not only been redeemed *from* hell and eternal separation from God; we are redeemed *to become* joint heirs with the Lord Jesus (Romans 8:15-18). The major emphasis in redemption is not the former but the latter. It is important to grasp the terrible magnitude and consequences of man's fall, but it is far more important to understand the magnificent consequences of redemption. It is here the emphasis in training is to be focused; that is, to find the purpose of God for one's life and be committed to it.

This we must do now; it is not a matter of waiting to see what the next life may have for us. We are to discover and embrace the call for which we have been apprehended. This will form the basis for guidance in all areas of our life, such as marriage, profession, etc. What we become in Him during this present life, through the power and grace of God, determines the glory and place we have in His kingdom to come. To that end, *all* that we will ever need for godly character or service is available to us through the Holy Spirit. Being filled with the Spirit is not a gateway to instant victory. In many ways it will accentuate our warfare, for through it boundaries become more clearly defined. The power of the indwelling Spirit does not remove any responsibility to exercise our wills. If we will heed the quiet, inner voice of the Spirit, and not follow the dictates of our senses, emotions and reason, we can experience the joy of victorious living. If we walk in the Spirit we will not fulfill lusts of the flesh. We live in two worlds, one of the Spirit and one of the flesh. The position of the soul, between the spirit and body in our graphic model, serves to illustrate this truth. The issue is how, in the exercise of our wills, we use the inputs from these two realms to govern our lives.

The Work of the Cross

The gospel is made up of three vitally important truths: the death, the burial and the resurrection of Christ (1 Corinthians 15:1-4). This is why the gospel is called the gospel of the glory of Christ (2 Corinthians 4:4). A major step toward a victorious Christian life is learning to appropriate *all* that Christ provided for us in His death, burial and resurrection, which are totally sufficient to deal with the sins and failures of our old nature.

Through death on the cross, Jesus shed His blood to forgive the sins of all who have faith to repent and believe in Him. Only His blood can forgive our sins!

In the Old Testament, the blood of animal sacrifices atoned for the sins of the people. These animal sacrifices were required as often as the people sinned. However, there always remained an inner consciousness of sins, for although their sins were covered, men's consciences were not cleansed; their sins and failures were never forgotten.

Jesus was conceived by the Holy Spirit in the womb of Mary. After birth, He lived a completely sinless life. The blood in His veins was the blood of a perfect sacrifice. He was the unblemished Lamb of God, the sacrifice for sins, whose blood not only covered sins, but also totally forgave them so that they are never remembered again by God (Hebrews 10:1-18). Thus, believers need not bear a continual consciousness of past sins; their consciences have been cleansed by the blood of Christ and they can always draw near to God in full assurance of faith (Hebrews 9:14).

The word "justify" is translated from the Greek word "DIKAIOO" which means "to declare righteous." To pass from death into life is only possible when one has faith in the shed blood of Christ to forgive all of one's sins. This truth is expressed in the following scriptures.

> *Therefore having been* ***justified by faith*** *we have peace with God through our Lord Jesus Christ . . . Much more then, having been* ***justified by His blood,*** *we shall be saved from the wrath of God through Him. (Romans 5:1, 9)*

> *Knowing that you were not redeemed with perishable things . . . but with* ***the precious blood*** *as of a lamb unblemished and spotless,* ***the blood of Christ.*** *(1 Peter 1:18-19)*

Just as it requires faith to believe that the shed blood of Christ forgives our sins, it also requires faith to believer the scriptures concerning our old nature.

> *Even so,* ***consider*** *(reckon, fully believe)* ***yourselves to be dead to sin,*** *but alive to God in Christ. (Romans 6:11)*

It is a moment-by-moment reckoning ourselves to be dead to sin and alive to God in Christ. What is dead, cannot sin! If I truly believe that my "old nature" is dead indeed to sin, *then by faith* I can live the new life which all true believers receive in Christ through the new birth! Salvation is truly living an exchanged life; I have died and Christ now lives in me. Paul expressed it this way:

> ***I have been crucified with Christ;*** *and it is no longer I who live, but Christ lives in me; and the life which I now live in the flesh* ***I live by faith*** *in the Son of God, who loved me, and delivered Himself up for me. (Galations 2:20)*

Jesus died on the cross and was buried as the last Adam to deal once and for all with the Adamic nature!

How is this important truth proclaimed in the gospel and how do new converts appropriate it by faith? The answer is found in the *waters of baptism!* The first step by which a new beliver expresses his faith in this truth is to personally participate in the Lord's *burial by being baptized in water*. In doing so, he is testifying, "I believe that my old-self was crucifed with Jesus on the cross, and I now bury it in the waters of baptism, where the Holy Spirit will cut it away by circumcision so that I may rise out of the water to walk in newness of life."

The waters into which one is immersed do nothing; what takes place is a work of the Holy Spirit.

The following scriptures, which proclaim this truth concerning the burial of Christ, are where our faith is to be fixed.

> *Therefore* ***we have been buried with Him through baptism into death,*** *in order that as Christ was raised from the dead through the glory of the Father,* ***so we too might walk in newness of life.*** *For if we have become united with Him in the likeness of His death, certainly we shall be also in the likeness of His resurrection,* ***knowing this, that our old self was crucified with Him, that our body of sin might be done away with, that we should no longer be slaves to sin.*** *(Romans 6:4-6)*

Notice that the promise is neither regeneration by baptism nor sinless perfection, but of victory over habitual sin. Sin is *not* to be our master. We can walk in victory!

> *In Him also you were circumcised with a circumcision not made with hands, but in a (spiritual) circumcision (performed by) Christ by stripping off the body of the flesh (the whole cor-*

rupt, carnal nature with its passions and lusts). (Thus you were circumcised when) you were buried with Him in (your) baptism . . . . (Colossians 2:11-12; Amplified Bible)

The death and burial of Jesus in the gospel involved His humanity; His resurrection revealed His deity.

Having been spiritually born into God's family, the gospel promise of His resurrection is the promise of power in the Holy Spirit to serve the Lord and to spiritually grow into His likeness. We identify with His resurrection by being baptized in the Holy Spirit (Acts 1:8; 2:38; 10:44-48; 19:1-6). It is a valid expectation to see believers filled with the Holy Spirit when they come up out of the waters of baptism.

Jesus was not only the last Adam, He was also the first-born from the dead, the first of a new race of beings of which He is the head. Scripture speaks of this people as "the body of Christ" or the church. It is the collective spiritual relationship of all those in union with Christ; this is where each believer finds his identity and place of service. All fruit, all gifts, and all ministry come from the Holy Spirit. There is a unique deposit of His spiritual life within each one of us that determines our call in His body. He is to be center focus in all things! This organism of spiritual life is not based on religious organization. It is simply the life union that each believer has with Christ, and thereby with one another, to become a living body under His headship.

God's witness of what He has done for us in the death, burial and resurrection of His Son is the threefold witness of the blood, the water and the Spirit (1 John 5:6-7).

From the time of a child until He gave up His spirit on the cross, Jesus lived a life of choice. Every decision He made was a disciplined choosing between what He received from the window of physical senses and from the window of spiritual senses (the Holy Spirit). The fact that He did not sin was not because He could not sin, being God; but because he chose not to. He was made as a man with a free will to choose. He was tempted in all the ways we are, and thus, He came to know our human weaknesses. Because of this, as our High Priest, He faithfully intercedes for us. Moreover, He set the example for us on how to walk in righteousness. In the manner He overcame, we can also overcome through the guidance and power of His Spirit. To yield our will to Him, is to recognize that we have been crucified, our old nature was put to death at Calvary, and our new nature is now the Lord himself living within us. This is the way of victory; it is the law of the Spirit of life in Christ Jesus!

These fundamental truths concerning the cross are foundation stones to build lives in righteousness. If they are not taught and practiced, the door will be opened to legalism, which is how the carnal mind of man seeks to establish righteousness. Legalism produces slaves; grace produces disciples!

Renewal of Our Minds

Ways of our old nature do not pass away immediately after we are saved. God exhorts us in His word to lay aside our carnal way of life and be renewed in the spirit of our mind (Ephesians 4:22-24). The option we face is either be conformed to this world, or be transformed by the renewal of our minds.

The sin of Eve in the garden of Eden came to pass because of Satan's attack on her mind. Her response was self-centered, and the spiritual damage that she incurred has been passed down to all succeeding generations. Because Eve believed a lie, our human mind-set is to live that lie. We want to appear wise and godly. We would sooner expound doctrines and theories than be honest and face the reality of our false fronts. However, the real person that we are lives behind the facades and pseudo-spiritual lives that we present to others. This is where change must come!

Renewal of one's mind is not a matter of education; it requires a divine work of the Holy Spirit that touches our mind and our spirit.

Satan cannot read our mind, but he can and does bring thoughts into our mind. How we respond is key! Our mind is the primary battleground upon which we fight the good fight for a victorious life in Christ. The battle is to bring our thought life into obedience to the will of God. The weapons of our warfare, our understanding, our ability to minister, all come from the anointing of the Holy Spirit on our spiritual senses. The reality of His anointing transcends by far what one could experience by education through natural senses. The following scripture describes the spiritual battle that marks the process of renewal.

> *. . . for the weapons of our warfare . . . are divinely powerful for the* ***destruction of fortresses.*** *We are destroying speculations and every lofty thing raised up against the knowledge of God, and we are taking every thought captive to the obedience of Christ. (2 Corinthians 10:4-5)*

Fortresses to be destroyed are those thoughts brought into minds, which when accepted and acted upon will cause one to sin against God or against brothers and sisters in the body of Christ. If not destroyed, such fortresses can lead to demonic activity. Some examples of fortresses are unforgiveness, fear, pride, self-contempt, jealousy, envy, hatred, lust, racism, resentment, etc. Renewal of our minds requires honesty in facing such traits. This aspect of redemption, which certainly requires the power of God, is best accomplished in a covenant relationship of friends in Christ. There can be faithful surgery in the wounds of a friend!

The essence of a renewed mind is one whose thought life has come under control, where there is a submissive spirit to the authority of Christ. His government is the sword that divides men. His peace exists wherever He governs; and the ones who He governs are the ones He will change.

The following four properties, in particular, mark a renewed mind:

1. A mind whose thought life is under the government of Christ; one who is at peace with out turmoil or anxiety (Philippians 4:6-9; Isaiah 26:3).

2. A mind that exhibits the trait of humility.
   True humility is to see oneself just as the Lord sees us. This means having no confidence in one's ability or self. However, it also means recognizing that we are God's sons seated with Him in heavenly places (Ephesians 2:4-10).

3. A mind which has accepted forgiveness from God, and which freely extends forgiveness to others both for past and present wrongs suffered.

4. A mind with a deep desire to know the Lord and His ways better (Philippians 3:10-15). Once we become satisfied with where we are, we begin to backslide. The better we know Him, the greater this desire will be. A renewed mind is Christ-centered, not self-centered.

Sin, Sickness and Health

Although all sicknesses are not the direct result of some specific sin, it is apparent that sickness and disease do have their origin in the sin of Adam. It is also clear in scripture that the wounds of Christ in His scourging provide for physical healing (Psalm 103:2-3; Isaiah 53:4-5; 1 Peter 2:24).

This raises the question, "How should believers pray for healing; how does one appropriate divine health?"

The first step is certainly to take advantage of what is available to us in the physical realm, such as nutrition, rest, exercise and medical services. However, our wholeness is more than just a physical issue, it involves our spirit and soul as well.

In his third epistle, John links good health in the body to good health in the soul.

> *Beloved, I pray that in all respects you may prosper and* ***be in good health, just as your soul prospers.*** *(3 John 1:2)*

In his epistle to Thessalonica, Paul recognized that one's body, soul and spirit are woven together to form a living whole being, and he prayed that *each* part of the whole person would be preserved complete and without blame. Sanctification involves body, soul and spirit.

> *Now may the God of peace Himself sanctify you* ***entirely;*** *and may your (whole) spirit, soul and body be preserved* ***complete,*** *without blame . . . (1 Thessalonians 5:23)*

The second step in answering our question is to understand the relationship that may exist between sin and disease. The following scriptures imply that there is a causal relationship: Exodus 15:26; Deuteronomy 28; John 4:14 and 1 Corinthians 11:27-31. Some obvious examples are lung cancer and smoking, cirrhosis of the liver and alcoholism, venereal disease and sexual sin. David's repentant words in Psalm 38 reflect a causal relationship between his health and sin that he had committed.

> *There is no soundness in my flesh because of Your indignation; there is no health in my bones because of my sin. (Psalm 38:3)*

However, what about sin that is not of the flesh? Do we really understand the important role that our spirit and soul play in our physical health? We may not be able to quantify it, but there is great therapeutic value to our physical well-being from joy, laughter and peace. On the other hand, who knows what sickness can arise from the presence of resentment, bitterness and strife in a person's spirit?

> *A joyful heart is good medicine, but a broken spirit dries up the bones. (Proverbs 17:22)*

The field of medicine describes some sicknesses as being psychosomatic (symptoms in the body and/or the mind as a result of a mental condition). I suspect that this classification may be the tip of a great iceberg!

Consider the battle to control our thought life, and Satan's strategy to deceive us and cause us to sin. If we accept and harbor thoughts that he brings into our mind, we will sin. We commit the sin of unbelief if we do not hold fast to what God has declared in His word to be true concerning our relationship to Him and to His body. The following are some possible scenarios of such sin.

- Failure to walk in the light of God's revealed grace and His word concerning our position in Christ can lead to self-contempt, great guilt, spirits of depression and hopelessness. Sickness and even suicide could eventually result.
- The sin of unbelief can give rise to fear, anxiety and stress that could result in sicknesses such as ulcers and hypertension.
- The sin of unforgiveness can produce inner tensions of hurtful memories that could cripple one's health as well as destroy relationships in the body of Christ.

In summary, I suspect that the state of one's spirit and soul is a much more important factor for good physical health than most Christians realize. Our outer man reflects what is on the inside, which is where our focus should be.

Watch over your heart with all diligence, for from it flow the springs of life. (Proverbs 4:23)

To complete the answer of how believers are to pray for healing, it is clear that such ministry should include both counsel and prayer. Before praying in faith for healing, any evidence of sin from strongholds or fortresses, that may be present in the afflicted one's mind, should be dealt with. This could include deliverance from demons. The following scripture, that concerns prayer for the sick, points clearly to the possibility of sin being a cause of sickness.

> *Is anyone among you sick? Then he must call for the elders of the church and they are to pray over him, anointing him with oil in the name of the Lord; and the prayer offered in faith will restore the one who is sick, and the Lord will raise him up,* ***and if he has committed sins, they will be forgiven him. Therefore, confess your sins to one another, and pray for one another so that you may be healed*** *. . . . (James 5:14-16)*

Faith and the Word of God

To accept God is to accept His word; to reject His word is to reject Him. Our faith in Him is supported by how He has revealed Himself and His purposes to us in the scriptures. It is not primarily teaching about the Lord we need, but time spent in His presence. And we need simple faith to embrace what He reveals to us (1 Corinthians 2:1-16). Above all, we must recognize that our faith is *in Him, not in our knowledge of the Bible.* Our faith is to be in the Author of the word. It is possible to know the Bible well and yet not know Him.

The tastes and habits that each of us possess are developed over time. They are not inherent in our nature. So it is with acquiring a good knowledge of the scriptures; we must cultivate a love for the Bible through diligent study. Jeremiah expressed it this way:

> Your words were found and I ate them, and ***Your words became for me a joy and the delight of my heart*** . . . . (Jeremiah 15:16)

His character, His ways and His purposes never change; therefore, His word is also unchanging. As we know Him better, we will find His word to be an ever-unfolding revelation of His nature, glory and will. To memorize the Bible without cultivating a deeper relationship with the Lord has little value. Jesus is the author and perfecter of our faith; He is the basis of faith in all matters. It is He, not simply the letter of the word that is the basis of our faith. Because He is eternal, His word is also eternal.

> *The grass withers, the flower fades, but the word of our God stands forever. (Isaiah 40:8)*

> *Forever, O Lord, Your word is settled in heaven. (Psalm 119:89)*

> *Heaven and earth will pass away, but My words will not pass away. (Matthew 24:35)*

The Lord honors His word as He honors His own name since it is an expression of His person and purpose. To love the Lord is to love His word; and to love His word is to obey it.

A seed contains within it all the properties of the mature plant that will one day grow from it. So it is with the word of God. We receive the implanted seed of the gospel into our hearts at conversion. If the soil of our heart is good, the nature of Christ will grow within us.

> *For you have been born again not of seed which is perishable but imperishable, that is, through the living and enduring word of God (1 Peter 1:23).*

To grow spiritually and manifest the nature of Christ in one's life requires a discipline of prayer and systematic study of the word.

We are saved through faith, and without faith it is impossible to please God. Thus, it is important to recognize the place that scripture has in developing faith.

> *. . . Faith comes from hearing and hearing by the word of Christ. (Romans 10:17*

Although the scriptures are the inerrant word of God, our understanding and interpretation of the Bible may be incorrect, or at least incomplete. It is a great error to try and manipulate God by using His word to obtain a result we desire. We may sound spiritual in our prayers: "Lord, your word promises this, therefore You must do it." However, our declarations of faith and strong prayers will avail little if we do not know His heart in the matter. Seeking Him is *always the first priority*. When He quickens a portion of His word to us, that is where our faith is to be applied. We are to seek *Him* and His ways, and *commit to Him* the work of His hands. The prophet Isaiah expressed it well:

> *. . . Ask Me about things to come concerning My sons, and you shall* ***commit to Me*** *the work of My hands. (Isaiah 45:11)*

The reason why the Holy Spirit must reveal the word for us to be certain of interpretation and understanding is because He knows the mind of God and He is the Spirit by whom the scripture was written. We can be introduced to an author by reading his book, but only if we come to know the author well will we truly understand his writings. Thus, through knowing Jesus, the living Word of God, we will understand the scriptures and have a solid basis for our faith.

Jesus said His words are spirit and life (John 6:63). It is not the letter which brings life, but God's anointing upon His word. Too much emphasis on spiritual gifts to the neglect of teaching and studying the scripture can lead to walking by experiences; too great an emphasis on the word, without properly recognizing the ministry of the Holy Spirit, can produce a state of religious legalism. Balance comes out of the strength of a personal relationship to Jesus. It is Jesus we are to seek; to know Him is to know balance. The sword of the Spirit is what we are equipped with as soldiers of Christ. For although we are a covenant family, we are also a disciplined army engaged in spiritual warfare.

> *And take . . . the sword of the Spirit, which is the word of God. (Ephesians 6:17)*

What God purposes to do through His people can only be accomplished by His power and grace. It is difficult to grasp the magnitude of this grace. We were saved by grace when deep in transgressions. By grace He made us alive together with Christ, and seated us with Him in heavenly places. By grace He is fashioning us into His image; and by grace He has prepared works for restoration, harvest and judgment that He will accomplish in the earth through us in these last days.

Finally, He will display the riches of His grace in kindness toward us to all creation in the age to come (Ephesians 2:4-10).

Consequences of Redemption

The fall of man was the result of believing Satan's message of "promotion of self; do your own thing." This is the spirit of self-will that is in the world today.

The redemption of man is based on the gospel of the kingdom which declares, "I love you, and I have paid the price for your sins of rebellion. Receive My forgiveness and come into My kingdom under My government; deny yourself and do My will."

The primary consequence of redemption is the central and preeminent place that Jesus is to have in the life, service and purpose of the redeemed. He must be seen for *who* He is; One in whom the fullness of Deity dwells in bodily form and whose name is above every name. One who is before all things and in whom all things hold together. He is the radiance of His Father's glory and the exact representation of His nature. He is also head of the body, the church where He merits first place in everything. He is Lord of lords and Kings of kings! The government is upon His shoulders!

The commission given to Adam to rule the earth will be extended to the redeemed of the Lord. Just as in the case of Adam, we can only rule through spiritual union with the Lord. Union is possible because the shedding of His blood is sufficient for the cleansing of *all sin for anyone* who comes to Him in faith. In addition, the spilling of His blood on the soil will, in the end, remove all effects of the curse from the earth. Finally,

Jesus took the keys of death and Hades from Satan. Those who respond to the gospel of grace and become subject to the Lordship of Christ, are no longer under the authority of the prince of this world.

What transpires within us between redemption and when we reign with Christ, is essentially a preparation for glory. The primary objective today is the same as it has always been: to become like Jesus.

We have to lay aside our desires for self-fulfillment. Our heart focus has to shift from ourselves to Christ, seeking to know Him more intimately. Not simply for the work of His hands in miracles, but for His presence. Paul's prayer for the believers at Ephesus expresses it well:

> *That the God of our Lord Jesus Christ, the Father of glory, may give to you a spirit of wisdom and of revelation in the knowledge of Him. **I pray that the eyes of your heart may be enlightened,** so that you may know what is the hope of His calling, what are the riches of the glory of His inheritance in the saints, and what is the surpassing greatness of His power toward us who believe . . . . (Ephesians 1:17-19)*

Truth begins with the spirit of revelation touching our spiritual senses to reveal the person and will of Christ to us.

Chapter 4

Education And Revelation

Mind Over Matter and Spirit Over Mind

To discover the purpose of God for our lives, we must first obey Him in the simple practical things of every day living. Secondly, He must be sought. He is a God who hides Himself, and only those who seek Him will fathom His ways. Our call will become apparent to us as we grow in our knowledge of Him.

One essential difference between us and the animal world lies in our ability to think and derive understanding through education. Animals can only be trained; humans can also be educated. However, a much greater difference is the spiritual faculty by which we know God. This dimension of knowledge is unique to the Holy Spirit. It is the phenomenon of revelation. We are educated via the window of natural senses, but we only know the Lord through the Spirit of revelation via our spiritual senses. Whereas a good mind is required to acquire education, a humble, teachable, guileless spirit is the secret in learning the mysteries of God. One may generalize by stating that animals live by their senses, unsaved mankind lives by his mind and the Christian lives by his spirit. Figure 6 illustrates the processes of education and revelation.

It is sad to see scientific men and women link their genesis to the animal world, instead of to the One who created them in His likeness. They do so because their spirit is dead. Being separated and alienated from God, they lack insight into the realm of His being. We find God when we seek Him with all our hearts and when, by grace, He reveals himself to us. A necessary step is

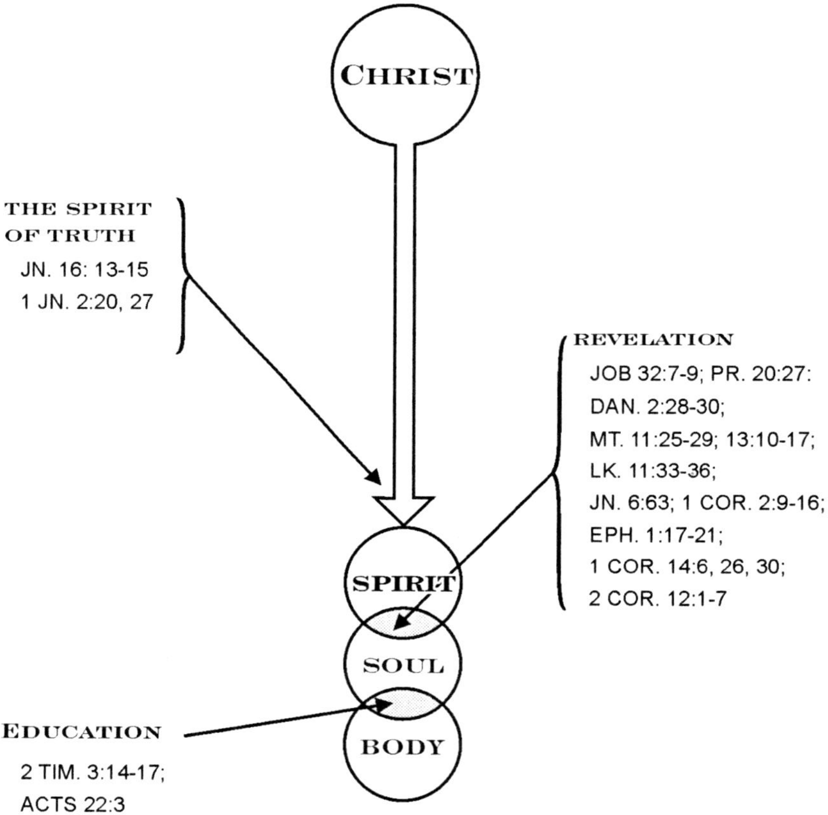

EDUCATION & REVELATION

FIGURE 6

always revelation. First the revelation that, although we are lost, He loves us even in our sin and has provided the way back for us to again have fellowship with Him. The revelation that undergirds all other revelation is the revelation of His person. Who He is, the glory of His character and the great love He has demonstrated for us on the cross, takes precedence over any other revelation.

What is Truth?

In our humanity we seek truth through the window of our physical senses. We apply our mind in rational thinking, philosophy and reasoning to what we experience and what our senses perceive, in order to know what, to us, is true. Truth is simply whatever we prove or believe to be true.

However, once we become a child of God we discover that truth is a Person (John 14:6)! Through our spiritual senses, as we grow in our relationship with Him, we experience through the spirit of revelation what truth really is (John 16:13). It is not related to logic or rational thinking; it is knowing Christ!

It is easy to accept the validity of what is received through physical senses; however, truth in the fullest sense of the word, are those things revealed by the Spirit of God. For example, it is scientifically true that water is made of hydrogen and oxygen; it is spiritually true that Jesus made water out of hydrogen and oxygen, and sustains it by the word of His power. Thus, truth is more than correct facts. A proud, haughty spirit will not hear from God, for He reveals himself to those who are lowly of heart and poor in spirit. How can a revelation be accepted as truth when it involves things not proven by a demonstration of logic and reason on our part?

There is an inner witness of the Spirit when truth is in harmony with God's word. An unqualified acceptance of revelation is a very real act of faith and there must be a solid foundation for such faith. This foundation is the word of God.

Revelation may occur when reading scripture and a portion is quickened (or made alive) to us. Revelation may also come to us in dreams, visions, prophetic words or through personal, inner impressions. However it occurs, revelation will never be contrary to the written word.

The still, small voice of the Spirit can speak to us when we are not reading the scriptures. He may awaken us and speak to our hearts during the night hours; or a word may come as we reach out to Him for understanding and help during a problem or set of circumstances we are facing. Revelation may burst into our understanding while we are listening to someone preach. It may also occur as we observe some simple event, and the Lord speaks to our heart concerning a spiritual principle. Regardless of how revelation comes, it is the beginning of *all* spiritual truth we possess. Since Jesus is *the truth*, the ultimate purpose of revelation is to reveal Him.

All we will ever need to know as children of God is found in Him; to know Christ is to know the mystery of God.

> *. . . All the wealth that comes from the full assurance of understanding, resulting in a true knowledge of God's mystery, that is,* ***Christ Himself****, in whom are hidden* ***all*** *the treasures of wisdom and knowledge. (Colossians 2:2-3)*

Finally, there is an environment for revelation and it is not being in a seminary or Bible school; it is simply being in His presence with a hungry heart.

The Place of Education

Education is *not* an alternative to revelation. It is possible to memorize the entire Bible and yet have no personal revelation of Jesus. Lack of revelation is a key reason why there are so many voices and divisions in Christendom today. Many believers have grown dull of hearing because of too great an emphasis on knowing the letter of the New Testament and too little emphasis on the need for revelation. True orthodoxy is not only a matter of correctly interpreting the letter of the word, but also of placing proper emphasis on the qualities of one's heart. Knowledge can lead to arrogance, but a hunger for God and the spirit of revelation will establish one in Christ (1 Corinthians 8:1-3).

To hear and to accept uninspired theology as truth is to lay a false foundation for our faith. Some Christians sustain their faith from what they hear from tapes, read from books, or see on Christian TV programs. Such things are not necessarily wrong, but they must *never* take the place of revelation from the scriptures as a basis for our faith. Possibly the greatest snare in this area, especially to those in leadership, is the logic of making decisions based on how God has led in the past. Tradition can be a hindrance to revelation. It is easier to follow what worked yesterday than to seek the Lord for His direction today.

The relationship between truth and education is as follows: *education brings the logos (word) of God into one's mind; revelation quickens that word to our hearts, it becomes a rhema to us; once we know that a word is true, we are expected to obey it. Through obedience it becomes experiential truth* in our lives. In this way, we become testimonies of truth to the world. It is not primarily what *we believe*, but what *we are*, that makes us a light in darkness. The following transitions illustrate how scripture can become visible to others as truth in our life.

THE WORD>REVELATION>RHEMA>OBEDIENCE>TRUTH

God doesn't want us to discount intelligence, or minimize the training of our minds. He wants us to develop these faculties, but He wants it done out of a right heart relationship to Him. Education is necessary and good. However, to bring life, what we learn *must become truth* and not remain head knowledge. To be approved of God as a good worker with expertise in wielding the sword of the spirit, requires a diligent study of the scriptures on our part. We will never exhaust the truth it contains, nor will we ever exhaust our need for revelation.

The Spirit of Revelation

The Holy Spirit is the Revelator. His mission is to reveal the Lord Jesus and to glorify Him to us. All revealed truth will glorify and exalt the Lord Jesus Christ.

> *But when He, the Spirit of truth, comes, He will guide you into* ***all*** *the truth; for He will not speak on His own initiative, but whatever He hears, He will speak; and He will disclose to you* ***what is to come. He shall glorify Me;*** *for He shall take of Mine, and shall disclose it to you. (John 16:13-14)*

Revelation is simply the Holy Spirit teaching us. His anointing rests both upon the spoken (or written) word, and the ears which hear it. When there is no anointing, only information and concepts are passed on. Revelation is God's perspective of truth, given to us as we are able to bear it, line upon line and precept upon precept.

> *And as for you, the anointing which you received from Him abides in you, and you have no need for anyone to teach you; but as His anointing teaches you about all things, and is true and is not a lie, and just as it has taught you, you abide in Him. (1 John 2:27)*

> *It is the Spirit who gives life; the flesh profits nothing; the words that I have spoken to you are spirit and are life. (John 6:63)*

The Window of Revelation

Why is it often so difficult to embrace new truth? One cause comes from having received certain traditions as being truth, when in fact they are error. Conviction that is not founded on truth leads to error. It is not good when we are ignorant concerning a matter, but it is much worse when we believe we understand correctly and yet we are wrong. It is a tragedy when one who is deceived closes his heart to further instruction. The one sure safeguard is to keep our heart pure and open to the Lord so we will know His voice and be able to hear Him.

> *The lamp of your body is your eye; when your eye is clear, your whole body also is full of light; but when it is bad, your body also is full of darkness.*

Then watch out that the light in you may not be darkness. (Luke 11:34-35)

The most precious faculty we have is "spiritual eyesight," for if our "spiritual eye" is healthy our whole body will be filled with light. How well we grow spiritually is a matter of being swift to obey what is revealed to us. We cannot expect to receive new truth unless we put into practice what we have already been given. To turn away from revealed truth is to turn toward darkness. The above verses use the word "eye" to describe one's capability to understand or see spiritual things; this figure of speech refers to our window of the spirit.

But it is a spirit in man, and the breath (Spirit) of the Almighty gives them understanding. (Job 32:8)

A spirit open to new truth is like a lamp which the Lord can "turn on" to reveal understanding and truth.

The spirit of man is the lamp of the Lord, searching all the innermost parts of his being. (Proverbs 20:27)

The unfolding of Thy words gives light; it gives understanding to the simple. (Psalm 119:130)

Through revelation, the Bible ceases to be a dry history book with a lifeless philosophy, and becomes an exciting, day-by-day unfolding of the Lord and His purpose for us. Words, written two thousand years ago, become spirit and life to us today.

Only when the Holy Spirit brings scripture to life does it become sharp enough to divide and separate spirit from soul in one's understanding (Hebrews 4:12).

Without a present anointing of God's Spirit, Christian service will be confined to soulish endeavor; much activity but little life.

God hides treasures of His kingdom from the wise of this world, but reveals them to the simple, to those who are little esteemed by the world. He is not against human wisdom, but He *cannot* be found through it. He can only be known through revelation. We will not discover His treasures except out of the recognized poverty of our human talents. One who trusts only in his ability to reason and think will be spiritually dull. He assesses himself and the world around him on a soulish basis, where decisions rest on logic and reasoning. The window of spiritual revelation is closed to him. However, God has determined that *everything* concerning Himself and His kingdom is hidden from man, and can be *only* understood through revelation. Spiritual treasures must be sought for. We do not stumble upon them by accident. They are revealed to those who seek Him.

> *For nothing is hidden,* ***except to be revealed;*** *nor has anything been secret, but that it should come to light. (Mark 4:22)*

Flesh is flesh, and spirit is spirit. You can correctly interpret the flesh by the Spirit, but the reverse is *not* possible. Paul points this out in his epistle to the Corinthians:

> *. . . "Things which eye has not seen and ear has not heard, and which have not entered the heart of man,* ***all*** *that God has prepared for those who love Him." For to us God* ***revealed*** *them through the Spirit; for the Spirit searches all things, even the depths of God. For who among men knows the thoughts of a man except the spirit of the man,*

> *which is in him? Even so the thoughts of God no one knows except the Spirit of God . . . . But a natural man does not accept the things of the Spirit of God; for they are foolishness to him,* ***and he cannot understand*** *them, because they are spiritually appraised (or discerned). (1 Corinthians 2:9-14)*

One who trains and equips others is to be a living example of what he teaches. People may deny the word of God that is spoken to them, but they *cannot deny* what they see in the lives of His ministers. How we conduct ourselves can demonstrate truth to those we disciple. If we are not effective witnesses for Christ, either our message or our lives are not what they ought to be. Satan has deceived and blinded the minds of those who are lost, and only the light of revelation can penetrate their darkness.

> *. . . The god of this world has blinded the minds of the unbelieving, that they might not see the light of the gospel of the glory of Christ, who is the image of God . . . . For God, who said, "Light shall shine out of darkness," is the* ***One Who has shone in our hearts*** *to give the light of the knowledge of the glory of God in the face of Christ. (2 Corinthians 4:4, 6)*

It is sad to see a child born into the world without eyesight. Our hearts go out to such a person, knowing that they will never see the beauty of nature or the ones they love. However, it is even more pitiful to see men and women going through life unaware and unconcerned about their spiritual blindness. It is good to remember that we see by the grace of God; for only He can take away the veil from blind eyes and reveal himself. In Him is life, and this life is the light of men. What a privilege it is to see!

Chapter 5

Christian Character

What is Holiness?

Jesus is the radiance of His Father's glory and the exact *representation* of His nature (Hebrews 1:3). The Greek word for "representation" is CHARAKTER, from which our word character is derived. The literal meaning of this word is "a tool for engraving." Thus, to be fully conformed to the image of Christ is to be an exact engraved copy of Him. And this is our calling!

What does it mean to be holy? This is a very important question. Some would define holiness as the *absence* of sin. This is not correct; holiness comes from the *presence* of the Holy Spirit.

Once we are born again and receive the Holy Spirit, God calls us "saints", which means "set apart" or "holy." At this time, there is still much that needs to be changed in our life-styles and habits. Christ has come to dwell in our hearts; because of His presence within us, we are called "holy." Righteousness is not a passive absence of sin, it is the active presence of the life of God. Christian character becomes evident as we grow in godliness. The key word is change! One does not manifest perfect holiness at once, but grows in it through obedience.

Obedience begins with having faith in the promises of God's word.

> *For by these He has granted to us His precious and magnificent promises, so that by them you may become partakers of the divine nature, hav-*

> *ing escaped the corruption that is in the world by lust. Now for this very reason also, applying all diligence, in your faith supply moral excellence, and in your moral excellence, knowledge, and in your knowledge, self-control, and in your self-control, perseverance, and in your perseverance, godliness, and in your godliness, brotherly kindness. and in your brotherly kindness, love.* ***For if these qualities are yours and are increasing,*** *they render you neither useless nor unfruitful in the true knowledge of our Lord Jesus Christ. (2 Peter 1:4-8)*

The important thing is not how much stature we may have achieved; it is not where we are, but whether or not we are growing. One cannot stand still. To do so is to begin to backslide. Paul's heart-cry reflects the only attitude we can safely have for a victorious walk in the eyes of God.

> *Not that I have already obtained it, or have already become perfect, but* ***I press on in order that I may lay hold of that for which also I was laid hold of by Christ*** *. . . . I press on toward the goal for the prize of the upward call of God in Christ Jesus. (Philippians 3:12-14)*

Christian character begins and ends with the Holy Spirit; and it is corrupted by self-righteousness, by legalism and by sin.

The Place of Character

Character is developed within our spirits. Only the *Holy* Spirit can infuse holiness into us, and this begins in our spirits. This is where our likeness to God is developed. It will subsequently be seen in *how we think and what we do*, but character is what we *are* in our spirit. Spiritual union with God, which brings His righteousness into our hearts, is illustrated in Figure 7. This union is the basis of the law of the Spirit of life in Christ Jesus, the *one* law we are to walk in. What is in our heart (or spirit) defines our character; what comes out of our heart reveals our character. Thus, our first concern must always be for the state of our hearts.

> *Watch over your heart with all diligence, for from it flow the springs of life. (Proverbs 4:23)*

What we are in our hearts is how God sees us as individuals.

> *As in water face reflects face, so the heart of man reflects man. (Proverbs 27:19)*

David's prayer of repentance shows his recognition of this truth.

> *Create in me a* ***clean*** *heart, O God, and renew a* ***steadfast*** *spirit within me. (Psalm 51:10)*

Too often we think of sin as only what we *do* wrong, rather than the *attitude of heart* that leads us to sin. The scriptures make this distinction clear.

> *You have heard that it was said, "You shall not commit adultery" but I say to you, that everyone who looks on a woman to lust for her has committed adultery with her* ***already in his heart****. (Matthew 5:27-28)*

> *Everyone who hates his brother is a murderer . . . . (1 John 3:15)*

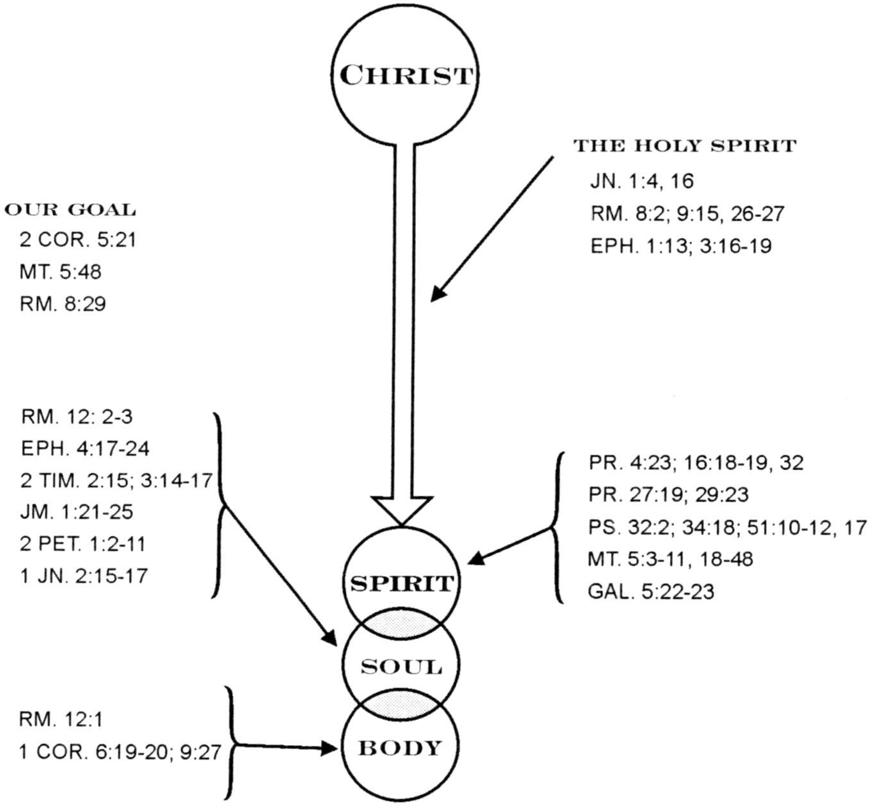

CHRISTIAN CHARACTER

FIGURE 7

To grow in righteousness, we need a humble, teachable spirit. There is no better counsel than our Lord's invitation:

> *Take My yoke upon you, and* ***learn of Me****, for I am* ***gentle and humble in heart****; and you shall find rest for your souls. (Matthew 11:29)*

The choice is ours, for we are masters of what comes into our hearts. Self-discipline is how we regulate what feeds our spirit. Neglecting to exercise control over our spirit will surely result in failure and sin.

> *Like a city that is broken into and without walls is a man who has no control over his spirit. (Proverbs 25:28)*

> *He who is slow to anger is better than the mighty, and he who rules his spirit, than he who captures a city. (Proverbs 16:32)*

The heart attitudes necessary to develop godliness are found in the Beatitudes (Matthew 5:3-8). The virtues of a godly character are fruits of the Spirit (Galatians 5:22). The one heart attitude to guard against, above all others, is pride. It is the father of all sin.

> *. . . clothe yourselves with humility toward one another, for God is opposed to the proud . . . . (1 Peter 5:5)*

In summary, Christ *in us* (in our heart) is our hope of glory; He is our righteousness (1 Corinthians 1:30)!

The Process of Character Development

Only God can change us; we are incapable of doing so by ourselves alone. However, we must be willing participants in the process. Character does not come as a consequence of experiences, valid though they might be; it comes from abiding in His life. The character of God cannot be separated from the life of God.

> *I am the vine, you are the branches;* ***he who abides in Me,*** *and I in him,* ***he bears much fruit;*** *for apart from Me you can do nothing. (John 15:5)*

> *In Him was life; and the life was the light of men. (John 1:4)*

The starting place is revelation; it begins with the word of life that penetrates our hearts. Our part is to obey the simple, basic truths concerning the person and work of Christ. This will draw us closer to Him. The better we know Him, the more we will want to be like Him and the greater our need will be apparent to us.

If we are faithful to keep our eyes upon Him while going through the problems in everyday experiences of church and secular life, we will begin to grow into His likeness. It requires much grace, for we will often fail. Many things will seem to hinder us. Indeed, we cannot grow in Him without growing in grace. The key is to always keep our eyes on Him, because the work of changing us is His, not ours. Progress will come by the grace of God through faith.

> *But we all, with unveiled face beholding as in a mirror the glory of the Lord,* ***are being transformed into the same*** *image from* ***glory to glory,***

> *just as from the Lord, the Spirit. (2 Corinthians 3:18)*

Any difficulties we encounter, such as persecution, privation, sickness, etc. will work character in us if we are able to see the hand of God in them. Our transformation will not be instantaneous but will involve times of transition in which there will be pain and struggle.

> *. . . but we also exult in our tribulations; knowing that tribulation brings about perseverance; and perseverance, proven character . . . . (Romans 5:3-4)*

It is only after going through problems and difficult times, that we can look back and see the good that was worked into us. Occasions of our human weakness are opportunities to draw on the Lord's strength (2 Corinthians 12:9-10)

> *. . . and that you, being rooted and grounded in love, may be able to comprehend with all the saints what is the breadth and length and height and depth, and* ***to know*** *the love of Christ* ***which surpasses knowledge, that you may be filled up to all the fullness of God.*** *(Ephesians 3:17-19)*

We cannot grow apart from knowing and responding to His love. It is God's love for us that reveals His character more than anything else. As we become like Him, we will reflect His love to all who belong to Him, and compassion for those in the bonds of Satan.

If we live and walk in the Spirit, our lives will naturally exhibit the fruit of the Spirit.

> *But the **fruit** of the Spirit is **love**, joy, peace, patience, kindness, goodness, faithfulness, gentleness, self-control; against such things there is no law. (Galatians 5:22)*

This love is a multifaceted expression of the character and nature of God, for above all else, He is love. That divine love is composed of many virtues becomes evident as we examine the above verse of scripture:

- Joy is love in *release*; it must be used for it cannot be preserved.
- Peace is love in *government*. Where He governs there will always be peace.
- Patience is love in *testing*.
- Kindness is love in *action*.
- Goodness is love displayed in *character*.
- Faithfulness is love in *commitment*.
- Gentleness is love in *concern*.
- Self-control is love in *discipline*.

> *Beloved, let us love one another, for love is from God; and everyone who loves is born of God and knows God. (1 John 4:7)*

> *But now abide faith, hope, love, these three; but the greatest of these is love. (1 Corinthians 13:13)*

A New Creation

There are seven biblical words that jointly define the new creation we become in Christ Jesus:

1. Repentance: a new will.

2. Regeneration: a new birth.

3. Justification: a new standing in righteousness.

4. Adoption: a new family relationship; we have become sons of God.

5. Conversion: new direction. The previous words all refer to a one-time-only experience. However, conversion is something we Christians encounter many times as our life is adjusted by the Lord.

6. Sanctification: new service. The quality level of our service will deepen as we grow in character.

7. Maturity: new stature in character and wisdom. This will become evident to others when our walk begins to match our words.

> *Therefore if any man is in Christ, he is a new creature; the old things passed away; behold, new things have come. (2 Corinthians 5:17)*

The transition that takes place within us in the process of spiritual growth comes from the change in our nature. Old things of the world are replaced by new things in His kingdom.

The Old and the New Natures

The process of this change involves putting off our old self (or old man) and putting on the new nature which *has already been created* in the likeness of God.

When Christ died on Calvary. He did more than shed His blood to wash away our sins. He also took our old nature with Him to the cross. It was nailed there to experience His death. *By faith* I must believe this, just as I believe that His blood washed away my sin. Being declared innocent through the forgiveness of my sin is one thing; however, recognizing that my old nature, which caused me to sin, has been put to death is quite another. This important truth is appropriated by a personal identification with His burial through water baptism.

The first apostles considered water baptism an important step in putting on the new nature. When we examine the New Testament record of the early church, we discover that water baptism *always* accompanied preaching of the gospel; it was never presented as an option, or as something to be done later at a more convenient time. The following are some examples from scripture.

> *But when they believed Philip preaching the good news about the kingdom of God and the name of Jesus Christ, they were being baptized, men and women alike. (Acts 8:12)*

> *And Paul said, "John baptized with the baptism of repentance, telling the people to believe in Him who was coming after him, that is, in Jesus." And when they heard this, they were baptized in the name of the Lord Jesus. (Acts 19:4-5)*

> *Surely, no one can refuse the water for these to be baptized who have received the Holy Spirit just as we did, can he: And he (Peter)* ***ordered them*** *to be baptized in the name of Jesus Christ . . . . (Acts 10:47-48)*

> *. . . Sirs, what must I do to be saved? And they said, "Believe on the Lord Jesus, and you shall be saved, you and your household." And they spoke the word of the Lord to him together with*

> *all who were in his house . . . and **immediately** he was baptized, he and all his household.* (Acts 16:30-33)

Abraham is the father of all who believe, because righteousness was imputed to him on the basis of his faith in God's promises. Faith was the basis for the Abrahamic covenant; this covenant is still in effect today through the Lord Jesus Christ, for He is the promised seed of that covenant (Romans 4:1-9; Galatians 3:6-16).

As a sign of their covenant, God required Abraham to take upon himself a *seal* of the covenant. This seal was physical circumcision, which was an act of physical cleanliness.

> *And he (Abraham) received the sign of circumcision, a **seal of the righteousness of the faith** which he had while uncircumcised* . . . . (Romans 4:11)

This circumcision was a type of the spiritual cleanliness we receive in the covenant today. In water baptism, the Lord circumcises the heart by "cutting away" the old man, which *by faith*, is buried in the grave of water. Before, during or immediately after, the candidate should be baptized in the Spirit. A walk in newness of life following baptism then becomes the seal (or sign) of the new covenant that we have embraced.

We recognize the wonderful promise of victory there is for converts in the death and burial of Christ! For everyone, but in particular, for those who are in the depths of sin, such as homosexuals or addicts to drugs, pornography, perversions, alcohol, tobacco, etc.; the gospel contains not only the promise of forgiveness of sins, but also the cutting away of such addictive bondages in our carnal nature by the Holy Spirit in the waters of baptism. All by repentance and faith!

Our "new self" is the Lord Himself, who lives in us through the Holy Spirit. We do not have a reformed old nature; we have a new nature, one created in true righteousness and holiness. From this nature comes the fruit of the Spirit. His life is our seal in righteousness (Ephesians 1:13; 4:30).

The choice is ours; we must choose to live by the Spirit and not be dominated by the senses of our soul-body window. The cross provides *all* that is necessary to live this new life, a life available to us through our spirit-soul window. But the choice is *always* ours. We choose which window dominates our life and conduct. Paul expressed it well in his epistle to the Romans.

> *For those who are according to the flesh* ***set their minds on the things of the flesh,*** *but those who are according to the Spirit, the things of the Spirit. For the* ***mind set on the flesh is death, but the mind set on*** *the Spirit is life and peace. (Romans 8:5-6)*

In summary, to put on the new self is to yield to Christ's life within us, for we have died and our life is now hidden in Him.

Part of the transformation we undergo in putting off the old self and putting on the new nature is a reorientation in our way of thinking. We need to be renewed in our minds. I must control my thought life, and recognize that I will not acquire the mind of Christ through head knowledge alone. I must daily present myself to Him as a living sacrifice, and seek His direction. It is a way of humility, but it is the *only way* I can walk with Him. We must be a people who spend much time in His presence at the throne of grace. If we fail to see our need in this area, we are surely headed for trouble (Hebrews 4:15-16).

> *I urge you therefore, brethren, by the mercies of God,* ***to present your bodies*** *a living and holy sacrifice, acceptable to God . . . . and* ***do not be conformed to this world, but be transformed by the renewing of your mind,*** *that you may prove what the will of God is, that which is good and acceptable and perfect. For through the grace given to me I say to* ***every*** *man among you not to think more highly of himself than he ought to think . . . . (Romans 12:1-3)*

> *. . . in reference to your former manner of life,* ***you lay aside the old self,*** *which is being corrupted in accordance with the lusts of deceit, and* ***that you be renewed in the spirit of your mind, and put on the new self,*** *which in the likeness of God has been created in righteousness and holiness of the truth. (Ephesians 4:22-24)*

The contrast between human judgment and the mind of Christ is greater than most of us realize. We are well-advised to take the following scripture at face value:

> *For My thoughts are not your thoughts, neither are your ways My ways . . . . for as the heavens are higher than the earth, so are My ways higher than your ways, and My thoughts than your thoughts. (Isaiah 55:8-9)*

A common weakness is our vulnerability to act or speak out of emotions. We make decisions and voice opinions based on how we feel, or how we are affected by circumstances at the time. When asked for counsel we are often quick to respond by quoting scripture. The mind of God says that at times of uncertainty we should do nothing; simply humble ourselves and pray for direction, and in due time the answer will be given to us. We are also prone to answer today's questions by what God said yesterday simply to have a ready answer. God is never in a hurry; when we speak or act in haste we are almost always in error. We cannot trust in our human reasoning; we need the mind of Christ!

Discipline

We all need help in the growth process. As children we benefited from the rod of correction in the hands of our parents. We required instruction in right behavior, but we also needed to learn from the consequences of our misbehavior. To be taught is one thing; to learn is something else.

Unfortunately, because of childhood experience, we tend to think of God's discipline as punishment for sin. This is not how to view it. His discipline is a training in righteousness; it is a mark of sonship.

> *For those whom the Lord loves He disciplines, and He scourges **every son** whom He receives . . . . He disciplines us for our good, **that we may share His holiness.** (Hebrews 12:6, 10)*

God's discipline can be found in the circumstances that we encounter with people and situations, as well as in His personal dealings in our lives. What comes into our life is there with God's permission, and He will not allow more than what we can bear. If we accept His discipline and learn from it, it will produce the peaceful fruit of righteousness within us. We are to welcome and embrace the discipline of God.

The experience of going through a period of time when God is dealing with us may be painful, but it can also have the wonderful result of building new dimensions of character into our lives. The key is to recognize that God is doing a good thing, and therefore we should embrace it accordingly and endure.

> *Behold, we count those blessed who endured. You have heard of the endurance of Job and have seen the* ***outcome of the Lord's dealings,*** *that the Lord is full of compassion and is merciful. (James 5:11)*

One purpose in such dealings is that the Lord can show His great love by bringing us through in victory. Each instance is a time of testing that refines dross from our lives as a furnace of affliction (Isaiah 48:10; Daniel 3:6-30).

> *And we know that God causes all things to work together for good to those who love God, to those who are called according to His purpose. (Romans 8:28)*

Whatever the circumstances may be, from time to time, we all will be tested. The secret of success is to not run from the situation *but to endure in faith*. In this way we will emerge into a place of abundance in Him. David expressed it well in Psalm 66:

> *For Thou has tried us, O God; Thou has refined us as silver is refined. Thou didst bring us into the net; Thou didst lay an oppressive burden upon*

our loins. Thou didst make men ride over our heads; we went through the fire and through the water; yet ***Thou didst bring us out into a place of abundance.*** *(Psalm 66:10-12)*

Second Childhood

It is remarkable how many messages are preached on the new birth and on Christian maturity, and how few are preached on one's second childhood. It is not possible to go from the new birth to being a mature person apart from growing up as a spiritual child.

We just naturally grow up physically, and we can judge our progress by age and to some extent by education. However, this is not true in the Spirit. Unfortunately, there are thousands who have experienced a spiritual birth, but have never progressed far beyond this state. On the other hand, there are some who grow up in Christ very quickly. Spiritual growth involves more than merely the time that one knows God.

Those who disciple, equip and oversee others must know how to relate to them during their growth phase, just as parents do in the develoP.M.ent of their children.

There are four well-defined levels of spiritual growth. The distinction between these stages can be seen in the meaning of the four Greek words that identify them in relevant scriptures:

1. *Brephos*—This word means "a newborn babe"; it describes one at the time of the new birth.

   Like ***newborn babes (brephos)*** long for the pure milk of the word, that by it you may grow in respect to salvation. (1 Peter 2:2)

The most important concern for "newborn" believers is that they have a hunger for the word of God, a hunger that should remain in them as they grow in the Spirit.

2. *Nepios*—This is the word which primarily identifies second childhood. It means a "minor," an "immature person," or a "child." The Holy Spirit has used *nepios* in the following scripture verses to provide insight into what to expect at this particular stage of growth. After the Lord gave authority to His disciples to heal the sick and cast out demons, they returned with joy to report their success. He told them not to rejoice in this, but to rejoice that their names were recorded in heaven; He then referred to them as babes in His prayer:

   At that very time He rejoiced greatly in the Holy Spirit, and said, "I praise Thee, O Father, Lord of heaven and earth, that Thou didst hide these things from the wise and intelligent and didst reveal them to ***babes (nepios)****" . . . . (Luke 10:21)*

   Thus, believers do not need to be mature to exercise authority over demons. This privilege belongs to any babe in Christ and is not related to spiritual growth.

   The following verses portray more clearly the character state of one who is a nepios:

   For everyone who partakes only of milk is not accustomed to the word of righteousness, for he is a ***babe (nepios)****. But solid food is for the mature, who because of practice have their senses trained to discern good and evil. (Hebrews 5:13-14)*

As a result, we are no longer to be ***children (nepios)****, tossed her and there by waves, and carried about by every wind of doctrine, by the trickery of men, by craftiness in deceitful scheming; but speaking the truth in love, we are to grow up . . . . (Ephesians 4:14-15)*

And I, brethren, could not speak to you as to spiritual men, but as to men of flesh, as to ***babes (nepios)*** *in Christ. I gave you milk to drink, not solid food; for you were not yet able to receive it . . . for since there is jealousy and strife among you, are you not fleshly? . . . for when one says, "I am of Paul," and another, "I am of Apollos," are you not mere men? (1 Corinthians 3:1-4)*

From these verses we see that a "nepios" will manifest some of the following faulty character traits:

- Inability to discern clearly between good and evil.
- Tossed around by the waves of circumstances and easily captivated by every new doctrine.
- Given to following after men rather than Christ, men with a desire for self identification in cliques, or men with a strong charismatic personality.

Such faults may seem bad but they are common in new Christians. Maturity takes time; growing out of them is what second childhood is all about.

3. *Neaniskos*—This word defines a young man in the prime of life. As in natural life, this is the stage that precedes fatherhood.

. . . I am writing to you, ***young men (neaniskos)****, because you have overcome the evil one . . . . I have written to you,* ***young men (neaniskos)****, be-*

cause you are strong, and the word of God abides in you . . . . (1 John 2:13-14)

Patience and love are required to guide *nepios believers* into this next stage of growth, which would correspond to "late teenage" in one's natural life. Such a person will show fruit from the Lord's discipline in his life. There will be a stability and faithfulness in his walk and service. He will become more like Jesus in word and deed.

When I was a child (nepios), I used to ***speak*** *as a child,* ***think*** *as a child,* ***reason*** *as a child; when I became a man, I did away with childish things. (1 Corinthians 13:11)*

4. *Pater*—This is the word for father (1 John 2:13-14). It denotes one who has matured sufficiently to father others in Christ; not just leading them to Christ, but becoming a father to them as Paul was to Timothy and to the Corinthian Christians (1 Corinthians 4:14-17). One cannot become a *neaniskos* or a *pater* without first being an accountable *nepios* and receiving love and instruction from tutors and fathers in the faith. This will build relationship.

There is a great need for spiritual fathers in the church today. A key period of training and preparation for all of us, is found in our "second childhood." To train and equip disciples without regard to where they are in their walk with God (i.e. recognizing the areas of their lives where there are problems) is clearly wrong. The process of developing character is described in 2 Peter 1:2-11. Here we see that it is a matter of faith in God's promises; it is not based on law.

Law and Righteousness

A tendency of human nature is to choose law as the way of righteousness. This is first seen in the history of Adam. Adam was informed that he could eat of *any tree* on the face of the earth that bore fruit having seed (Genesis 1:29). However, he was also told he could not eat of "the tree of the knowledge of good and evil." If he did so, he would die. It is apparent, therefore, the fruit of this particular tree had no seed. That is, it had no life within itself. It was a tree of death. In addition, Adam was also provided with the tree of life planted in the midst of the garden that he was to tend. The choice before Adam was explicit: choose life or death. When we examine the phrase: "knowledge of good and evil," we find it to be simply a definition of law. Law says, "This is good, that is evil: this is righteous, that is unrighteous." Therefore, the choice for Adam came down to one of choosing life or what would lead to law. And we know the choice that he made.

The story of Israel reveals the same mind-set. The nation was first given the privilege of receiving righteousness by faith in the covenant established with Abraham. Because the people did not walk by faith in this manner, and because of their many transgressions, God added the covenant of law made with Moses. This did *not* invalidate the earlier covenant (Galations 3:17). It placed before Israel a choice of either righteousness through faith in the Abrahamic covenant, or through obeying the law given to Moses. Again it was a choice of life or law, and we know the choice that they made. The Law was to be in effect as an obligation only until the promised seed (Christ) should come (Galations 3:19). The Law pointed Israel to the coming Messiah.

The same mind-set toward law was evident in the early church, as many who were justified by grace, sought to enhance their righteousness by keeping laws. This error was addressed by Paul, the apostle, in his epistles (Romans 14; 1 Corinthians 8; Galations 3; 4:1-11; 5:1-5; Colossians 2:20-23).Even the apostles, in the early part of their ministries, experienced some difficulty in totally breaking free from all Jewish traditions of law. The following are examples: Peter and Barnabas (Galatians 2:11-13); James (Acts 21:20-24) and Paul (Acts 18:18; 21:16). The Lord warned Paul not to go to Jerusalem because the Jews there would bind him if he did go (Acts 21:4, 10-11). This is precisely what happened; James and the other leaders persuaded Paul to purify himself through offering an Old Testament blood sacrifice. In this way they *bound him with bonds of the law* (Acts 21:18-26). It was the Romans who put him in chains. Although all of Paul's epistles contain the inerrant word of God, his epistles from jail provide a profound insight into the relationship of law and righteousness.

> *If you have died with Christ . . . why . . . do you submit yourself to decrees, such as,* ***"Do not handle, do not taste, do not touch!" . . . . These are matters which have, to be sure, the appearance of wisdom*** *in self-made religion and self-abasement and severe treatment of the body, but are of no value against fleshly indulgence. (Colossians 2:20-23)*

> ***Realizing the fact that law is not made for a righteous man,*** *but for those who are lawless and rebellious, for the ungodly and sinners, for the unholy and profane, for those who kill their fathers or mothers, for murderers and immoral men and homosexuals and kidnappers and liars and*

> *perjurers, and whatever else is contrary to sound teaching. (1 Timothy 1:9-10)*

A subsequent position of James is evident from his epistle, written near the end of his life, in which he calls freedom to choose righteousness as the perfect law (James 1:25; 2:12).

The tendency to set standards of righteousness in the church through laws has persisted until this day. Such laws vary by culture and denomination. Because of this, legalism is still a very real hindrance to the righteousness of God among Christians today. The relationship between law and true righteousness is clarified by the following set of questions and answers:

1. Is a requirement to keep the Law of Moses contrary to faith and spiritual life?
   Answer: Yes (Galations 3:10-14; Romans 3:20-28; 4:13-14)

   For, on the one hand, there is a setting aside of a former commandment (i.e. the law of Moses) because of its ***weakness and uselessness*** *(for the law made nothing perfect) . . . and on the other hand there is a bringing in of a better hope, through which we draw near to God. (Hebrews 7:18-19)*

2. Does not God's Law reveal His righteousness?
   Answer: No, it reveals the sinfulness of man (Romans 7:7, 13).

3. As Christians, what is our relationship to the Old Testament Law of God?
   Answer: All decrees against us, based on all commandments of the Law, were nailed to the cross of Christ, along with our old nature which

causes us to sin. This includes commandments related to the keeping of days and eating of foods. We are dead to the Law, and are released from it. The Law does *not* enter into our relationship with God today. Legalism weakens the conscience, and hinders the Holy Spirit's work of leading us to walk in His ways (Romans 7:4, 6, Galations 3:13, 23-29; Colossians 2:1-14).

*For Christ is the **end of the law for righteousness to everyone who believes**. (Romans 10:4)*

4. Are we to be without law?
   Answer: No, we are under the law of the Spirit of life in Christ Jesus (Romans 8:1-14; Galatians 5:16-18; Hebrews 8:8-13).

5. What are the characteristics of this law?
   Answer: It is not a law of obligation, but one of liberty with freedom of choice, whereby we *willingly choose* to walk under His guidance. He is to live His life in us; He is our righteousness. This is the *only* way the first commandment can be kept (James 1:25; 2:12; Galations 5:13-16; 6:2; 2 Corinthians 3:17-18).

6. Is there danger that we can abuse this liberty of choice?
   Answer: Yes (1 Corinthians 6:12; Romans 14:1-21; Galations 5:13-16)

7. What is the standard for righteousness:
   Answer: The righteousness of God. We are not to set standards for others, we are to be examples; Jesus is the *one and only* standard (2 Corinthians 5:21; Matthew 5:48; Ephesians 3:17-19).

The fact that law is useless to produce righteousness in a believer, does not mean that it is wrong or bad. Indeed, it is our human nature that is at fault not the Law (Romans 7:14). That is why law is intended for sinners so they can see the true state of their hearts. The Law is spiritual and holy since it came directly from the hands of God. It was given to make sin become utterly sinful. Thus, to deliberately break the commandments and teach others to do likewise, reveals a sinful heart. The Law was given to Israel as a tutor to prepare them for Christ. For the same reason, we are to teach our children the laws of God and raise them under parental discipline so that later, as adults, they will be willing to submit to the leading of the Holy Spirit within them and walk in a way pleasing to God. Since society is made up of largely unsaved people, its laws and legal system should reflect the commandments of God. In addition, when a believer in the church falls into sin and refuses to repent, he is placed under law so that he might repent and be forgiven (Matthew 18:15-17; 1 Corinthians 5:1-13; 2 Thessalonians 3:10). It is important to have the ten commandments displayed in public places, such as courts and schools, to discourage the spirit of lawlessness.

In summary, the character of a Christian expresses the extent to which Christ lives His life in that person. Clearly, while the potential is unlimited, the measure attained comes from a lifetime growth process that is orchestrated by God. Character is developed in one's spirit by the indwelling Holy Spirit and is reflected in the soul and body as believers freely lay down their wills to do the will of God. Their discipline for doing so is not from written law; it is the law of the Spirit of life in Christ Jesus.

Chapter 6

Our Priesthood

Called to Intimacy

The priesthood of all believers is one of the most important truths in scripture. Every true believer, by grace, has direct access to the presence of God through faith in the Lord Jesus Christ. There is no other intermediary nor special qualification. Priesthood is not reserved for a special class of believer. Every child of God is His personal possession, free to experience and proclaim His glorious excellencies. Freedom to serve God is the calling and privilege of each believer. Such serving is not an impersonal vocation, rather it flows out of an intimate relationship through prayer and worship which involves our whole person: body, soul and spirit (see Figure 8).

Ministry in His House

God expresses the calling which He has ordained for His people in several ways, as His sons, the bride for His Son and the body of Christ. Because of its frequency in scripture, the most significant representation of His purpose is probably that of us being the city or house for His habitation; the place of His eternal rest from which one day His glory will be fully and forever expressed to all creation.

There is a unique relationship between His house and our priesthood, something that is still being built today.

*You also, as living stones, **are being built up as a spiritual house for a holy priesthood**, to offer*

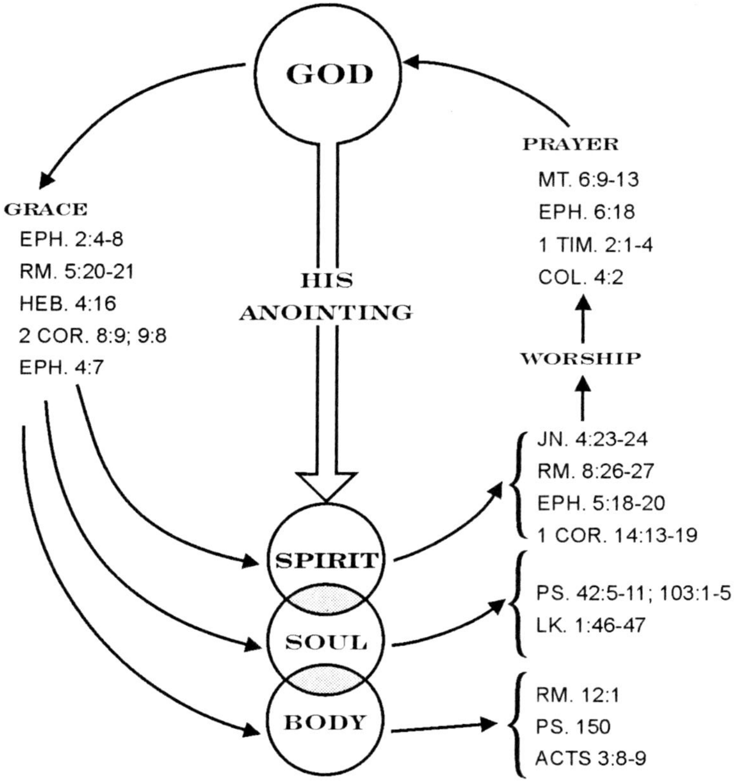

OUR PRIESTHOOD

FIGURE 8

up spiritual sacrifices acceptable to God through Jesus Christ. (1 Peter 2:5)

When we come into God's presence, worship is always the first priority. For this reason, our place in His house, first of all, is as priests. However, we do not worship simply as individuals; we are being built together as living stones in a corporate expression of worship.

There is no higher service than being a priest of God. The contribution of our sphere of service in the body of Christ and our growth of maturity in the Spirit, in the end, depends on the fruitfulness and the harmony of our roles as priests.

For the Lord has chosen Zion; He has desired it for His habitation. This is My resting place forever; here I will dwell, for I have desired it. I will abundantly bless her provision; I will satisfy her needy with bread. ***Her priests also I will clothe with salvation; and her godly ones will sing aloud for joy.*** *(Psalm 132:13-16)*

Our service as priests today is an apprenticeship for the age to come. Those who one day rule on the earth will be those who are faithful today as priests (Revelation 5:9-10). We learn to reign by spending time in His presence and coming to know the burdens of His heart; and we cannot be in His presence without worshipping Him. Prayer is how one develops the concerns of His heart. The practice of prayer, whether it is petitions, intercession or travail, helps to produce brokenness and humility.

Prayer

Scripture describes prayers of the saints as incense. In the Old Testament tabernacle, incense was made by beating together equal quantities of four spices. The resulting incense was stored in golden bowls until such time as the priest placed it upon hot coals of the altar. Only then was its fragrance released to arise into the air. This expresses an important truth. We are not to be discouraged when our prayers are not answered immediately. They are not lost or forgotten. They are stored in the golden bowls of God's memory. When His timing is correct, they will be placed on hot coals to release their fragrance; our prayers are then being answered (Revelation 5:8; 8:3-4)! Some of our prayers may not be answered in our lifetime, but they are just as important as those which are answered immediately.

We are called to be steadfast and faithful in prayer. We may not pray as long as others do, but we must be ready to pray at any instant. Prayer is the strategy of kingdom life (Matthew 6:9-15).

> *And they were* ***continually devoting*** *themselves . . . to prayer. (Acts 2:42)*

> *Pray without ceasing. (1 Thessalonians 5:17)*

Prayer is as necessary in support of spiritual ministry as breathing is to physical life.

Prayer is to be an expression of faith.

> *And all things you ask in prayer,* ***believing****, you shall receive. (Matthew 21:22)*

There is additional strength and faith when we pray together with others who are in agreement with us.

> *Again I say to you, that if two of you agree on earth about anything that they may ask, it shall be done for them by My Father who is in heaven. (Matthew 18:19)*

An important practice in prayer is to pray in the Spirit. Only the Holy Spirit knows the mind of the Lord. Thus, we need to pray with the spirit, as well as with our understanding. For example, prayer in the Spirit could be the Lord expressing His heart to break down barriers to the gospel in Islamic nations.

> *With all prayer and petition pray at all times in the Spirit, and with this in view, be on the alert with all perseverance and petition for all the saints. (Ephesians 6:18)*

> *. . . for we do not know how to pray as we should, but the Spirit Himself intercedes for us with groanings too deep for words; and He who searches the hearts knows what the mind of the Spirit is, because He intercedes for the saints according to the will of God. (Romans 8:26-27)*

> *What is the outcome then? I shall pray with the spirit and I shall pray with the mind also; I shall sing with the spirit and I shall sing with the mind also. (1 Corinthians 14:15)*

We are to be free from all unconfessed, unrepented sin when we come into His presence. We can only pray with confidence *if our hearts do not condemn us* (1 John 3:21-22).

If I regard wickedness in my heart, the Lord will not hear. (Psalm 66:18)

It is also necessary to be *honest* as we approach Him, for He will *not* tolerate hypocrisy (James 3:17). In prayer, we are not to represent ourselves as being in a place we have not yet attained. We may hide our true heart condition from one another, but there are no facades with God. If we are not honest, He will not hear us. He knows all about us, and it is vital for us to come to Him exactly as we are; repentant if necessary, but always in honesty. Additionally, we must come before Him from a place of forgiveness to others. He forgives us *if* we have forgiven those who offended us. There can be nothing in our hearts against even one of His children.

And whenever you stand praying, forgive, if you have anything against anyone; so that your Father also who is in heaven may forgive you your transgressions. But if you do not forgive, neither will your Father who is in heaven forgive your transgressions. (Mark 11:25-26)

Finally, God can only use broken men in His service, and prayer is a means of becoming broken. We will never build anything of quality apart from prayer!

Worship

True worshippers are those who worship the Father in Spirit and truth (John 4:23-24). Worship is much more a matter of recognizing His presence by the Holy Spirit's anointing on our spiritual senses than it is in how well we sing or how loud we shout. The following are four important qualities in how we are to present ourselves in worship.

1. *A Thankful Heart*—This quality concerns our heart attitude; a thankful heart must undergird all priestly activities. Thankfulness is more basic and important than other attitudes for it comes out of a recognition of who He is and what He has done for us

When one surveys the history of Israel, a major failure is seen in their frequent murmuring or complaining against the Lord and His servants. This practice is detested by the Lord, and we need to benefit from their experience (Numbers 14; Jude 16).

Now these things happened ***as examples for us****, that we should not crave evil things, as they also craved . . . . Nor let us try the Lord, as some of them did, and were destroyed by the serpents. Nor grumble, as some of them did, and were destroyed by the destroyer. (1 Corinthians 10:6, 9-10)*

Whether we are standing in a place of great abundance or in dire need; whether we are on top of a mountain or in a valley of despair; whether all is going well or we face a difficult situation, in *all* cases, we are to be thankful. Our heart attitude should not change because God does not change, and our hope and supply is in Him. Therefore, we are to come into His presence with thanksgiving.

Let us come before His presence with thanksgiving; let us shout joyfully to Him with psalms. (Psalm 95:2)

Enter His gates with thanksgiving, and His courts with praise. Give thanks to Him; bless His name. (Psalm 100:4)

Always *giving thanks for* ***all*** *things in the name of our Lord Jesus Christ to God, even the Father. (Ephesians 5:20)*

In everything *give thanks; for this is God's will for you in Christ Jesus. (1 Thessalonians 5:18)*

2. *A Sacrificial Heart*—This quality concerns what it costs to serve as a priest. It is apparent that self discipline is involved. One who serves must be willing to lay down feelings, and other things that they would sooner do, in order to minister to the Lord. In short, there is a sacrifice involving one's will, heart and body. *It costs something to serve as priests.*

   Through Him then let us continually offer up a ***sacrifice*** *of praise to God, that is, the fruit of lips that give thanks to His name. (Hebrews 13:15)*

   I urge you therefore, brethren, by the mercies of God, to ***present*** *your bodies a living and holy sacrifice,* ***acceptable*** *to God, which is your spiritual service of worship. (Romans 12:1)*

   There will arise situations and periods of discouragement when the last thing we will feel like doing is praising the Lord; however, it is during just such times that a sacrifice of worship on our part is required. Indeed, this is the way of victory. In many instances, situations are brought into our lives just to test our heart attitude and, when necessary, to adjust us through repentance. A humble, broken heart produces sweet worship in the Lord's ears. Brokenness of heart is a precious virtue!

The sacrifices of God are a broken spirit; a broken and a contrite heart, O God, Thou wilt not despise. (Psalm 51:17)

Animal sacrifices were tied to the altar during the Old Testament so they could not escape. However, the Lord Jesus willingly went as a lamb to be sacrificed for our sins. It is the same with us; only through a willing spirit can we offer up sacrifices. Worship is a *total* offering of ourselves; our bodies give expression in dancing or clapping, our souls (will, mind, emotions) magnify the Lord in hymns and song and, above all we worship in spirit and in truth from our hearts. We are to love Him with *all* of our heart, soul and strength, and to express this love in worship.

3. *A Hearing Heart*—This particular quality concerns hearing (or sensing) what the mind of the Lord is when in His presence. Priests are not in the rear of the Lord's army; they go before and show the direction set by our Commander-in-Chief.

   I appreciate so very much the role of worshipping musicians and other prophetic ministries in the assembly. The spiritual success of each meeting is centered in knowing the purpose and will of the Lord for that gathering, for He has a purpose whenever saints come together in His name. As we gather before Him, and minstrels lead forth in worship, His direction becomes known through the prophetic flow of word and song. There is to be a prophetic anointing on the congregation, including the minstrels to reveal this direction, just as there is an anointing on elders to oversee the meeting. This was the pattern for David's war strategy. Musical ability alone does not make acceptable worship; there must be a prophetic spirit as well, which can include visions.

Moreover, David and the commanders of the army set apart for the service some of the sons of Asaph and of Heman and of Jeduthun, who were to prophesy with lyres, harps, and cymbals. . . . (1 Chronicles 25:1)

Whenever we gather before the Lord, worship brings us corporately into His presence where He may speak and reveal His will to us.

Success in ministry is not a question of *knowing how* to do something, or *recognizing what* has worked in the past, but on hearing from heaven and moving accordingly.

4. *A Joyous Heart*—There is a great strength in spiritual joy which can only be found in His presence.

. . . in your presence is fulness of joy; in Your right hand there are pleasures forever. (Psalm 16:11)

. . . for the joy of the Lord is your strength. (Nehemiah 8:10)

His joy is totally unrelated to our feelings or circumstances. Satan is the author of fear and discouragement, but the joy of the Lord is our strength as we keep our eyes on Him and not on the problems and circumstances.

Worship is woven together by cords of joy and rejoicing to give us special strength during spiritual warfare and in situations of distress. At such times we *must* keep our eyes on Him, for if our eyes are on the problem we can miss the joy and strength that is in Him. *His* joy is our strength; it depends only on our relationship to Him (Isaiah 35:10).

So the ransomed of the Lord will return, and come with joyful singing to Zion; and everlasting joy will be on their heads. They shall obtain gladness and joy, and sorrow and sighing will flee away. (Isaiah 51:11)

Joy is our inheritance in Christ; we are to go in and out from His presence with joy, being led forth with peace to serve Him (Isaiah 55:12). The kingdom of God is *joy*, peace and righteousness.

Even in the midst of great difficulties, *by faith*, we are hidden in His tabernacle, our heads are lifted above our enemies and we can offer sacrifices with shouts of joy (Psalm 27:4-6). The city of God has walls of salvation and gates of praise. Ancient cities were protected by the strength of the walls around them. It was their salvation. However, gates were the means of life (food, etc.) flowing into the city. Gates of praise provide a life flow of joy for the city of God today.

But be glad and rejoice forever in what I create; for behold, I create Jerusalem for rejoicing, and her people for gladness. (Isaiah 65:18)

Therefore you will joyously draw water from the springs of salvation. (Isaiah 12:3)

Rejoice in the Lord ***always****; again I will say, re-* ***joice!*** *(Philippians 4:4)*

Joy is the language of worship!

The purpose of God is to establish His kingdom on earth. The essence of the prayer that Jesus taught His disciples to pray is, "Your will be done, on earth ***as it is in heaven***. (Matthew 6:10)

When we examine scripture to see what is happening in heaven, we discover the following: twenty-four elders cast their crowns before His throne and worship Him; four living creatures, on the sea of glass around the throne, worship Him; myriads of myriads and thousands of myriads of angels worship Him; every created thing in heaven and on the earth and under the earth and on the sea worship Him (Revelation 4:6-10; 5:11-13).

Jesus made it clear that His Father seeks worshippers.

But an hour is coming, and now is, when the true worshipers will worship the Father in spirit and truth; for such people the Father seeks to be His worshipers. (John 4:23)

It is apparent that becoming worshipers is how we are to prepare ourselves for the close of this age, and for the age to come.

Grace

We are saved by grace; by grace we grow in the Spirit; our service in the body of Christ is by grace, and our priesthood flows out of the grace of God. Our entire spiritual life is rooted in grace! Our High Priest,

Jesus, sits on His throne of grace, both interceding for us and ministering to us the grace that we need to be priests and ministries of the Lord. We are commanded to be strong in the grace of God!

As a young believer, I saw grace simply as God's condescension to save me; and once saved, it seemed to express His permissiveness for what I would be allowed to do within my testimony as a Christian. However, grace is not related to what we can do, it is related to what we are *not able to do*.

God's grace expresses His willingness to provided *all* we will ever need "to become" or "to do" what He has commanded us. The better we understand His purpose and plan for us, the more we will see our need for grace; the clearer we see the greatness of God and the weaknesses of our humanity, the more we can grasp the dimensions of that grace. Grace expresses the heart and the character of God in His free offer of all things pertaining to life and godliness.

Grace is extended to us according to His purpose for our life, and we appropriate it by faith. The wonder of it, is that *all* grace we will ever need was prepared for us before the world was made.

> *Who has saved us, and called us with a holy calling, not according to our own works, but according to His own purpose and grace which was granted us in Christ Jesus from all eternity. (2 Timothy 1:9)*

The most important call anyone can receive, the one from which all other aspects of His purpose for us emanate, is our call to be holy and blameless, being conformed to His image in character. There is nothing greater than this, *and only by grace can it happen!*

There is always more grace available to us than there is sin, weakness or failure on our part. Our victory lies in repentance and seeking grace to overcome when we fail.

> *. . . where sin increased, grace abounded all the more. (Romans 5:20)*

How is grace dispensed? Not in massive transfusions, but just as we need it, day by day. It is grace upon grace, upon grace, upon grace . . . .

> *For of His fulness we have all received and grace upon grace. (John 1:16)*

Because He foreknew our response to the gospel, He brings into our lives those circumstances and events that will most encourage us to make the correct decisions—decisions to help us grow and enable us ultimately to be conformed to the image of His son (Romans 8:28-32). Many of these circumstances are not pleasant to walk through, but we know they do work together for good to those who love God, to those who are called according to His purpose. These are the times when we must draw upon His grace. There is both pain and time involved in this transformation of our nature. It is a work that the Spirit of God must do; but it only happens with our willing consent and cooperation. This is where grace plays so important a role. Financial difficulties, the death of one dear to us, marital discord, problems with our employer, education or physical limitations—these all can be opportunities for the grace of God to work His character into us.

There will *always* be grace for each situation we face. His power is made perfect when it can be demonstrated in our personal weakness. Paul's "thorn in the flesh" was a weakness to him personally, but through grace it became a strength, for it helped prevent a character flaw of pride from coming into his life (2 Corinthians 12:7-10).

God does not give us grace after we have expended all of our ability; ministry is based on grace *from start to finish.* All ministry is an expression of the Lord's life, and therefore, of His grace. Our responsibility is twofold: first, to recognize our inability to perform; and secondly, to know that we are spiritually empowered. There is a unique relationship between the ministry and grace that we have been given. We cannot minister beyond the dimension of grace that is given to us. This is true, both for our ministries and our priesthood.

> *And since we have gifts that differ according to the grace given to us, let each exercise them accordingly . . . . (Romans 12:6)*

> *As each one has received a special gift, employ it in serving one another, as good stewards of the manifold grace of God. (1 Peter 4:10)*

When Paul left the elders of Ephesus, knowing he was seeing them for the last time, he commended them to God and the word of His grace. The Lord's word is not only truth, but it also carries His grace to help us possess truth. Jesus did not simply speak words of correct doctrine, He also spoke out of a heart of love that extended the help of His Spirit to bring the truth of His words to pass in those who received them. The law came through Moses, but grace and truth were brought by Jesus Christ.

For this reason, when we speak for Him our words must convey grace; we are to minister *truth and grace* when we speak. Too many words, or speaking with a wrong spirit can destroy grace.

> *Let no unwholesome word proceed from your mouth, but only such a word as is good for edification according to the need of the moment, that it may give grace to those who hear. (Ephesians 4:29)*

We are exhorted to make sure that no one in the assembly *comes short of the grace of God.*

> *See to it that no one comes short of the grace of God; that no root of bitterness springing up cause trouble, and by it many be defiled. (Hebrews 12:15)*

There are three simple keys involved in receiving grace. The first is that we will grow in grace as we grow in our knowledge of Him. The better we know Him, the clearer we will see His greatness and the more we will see our unworthiness and need of grace.

> *But grow in the grace and knowledge of our Lord and Savior Jesus Christ . . . . (2 Peter 3:18)*

The second key is that we only receive grace if our heart attitude is right. If we believe that we can make it on our own, we will be too proud to receive grace. Grace is only extended to the humble of heart.

> *. . . for God is opposed to the proud, but gives grace to the humble. (1 Peter 5:5)*

The third key is recognizing that grace comes *only* from the throne of God. It requires humility to approach His throne, and prayer is an attitude and expression of humility. Grace means something granted by "a greater" to those "who are lesser." Thus, prayer and worship mingled with faith, brings us to the source of grace.

> *Let us therefore draw near with confidence to the throne of grace, that we may receive mercy and may find grace to help in time of need. (Hebrews 4:16)*

The enemy of our souls continually points to our needs as the reason we will fail. God points to them as the reason why we will succeed, since He is our strength in them. Consider the dimensions of His supply:

> *And God is able to make* ***all*** *grace abound to you, that* ***always*** *having* ***all*** *sufficiency in* ***everything****, you may have an* ***abundance*** *for* ***every*** *good deed. (2 Corinthians 9:8)*

I *can* do *all* things through Christ who strengthens me.

We know from church history how God's grace has been sufficient for those who were persecuted and martyred for His name's sake. We have also seen how His grace has brought revivals of power and righteousness to the church from time to time. In the days that lie ahead, there will arise new dimensions of persecution and troubles to be faced by the church as she prepares for her Lord's return. At the same time, there will also be manifestations of the power of God upon His people as a great harvest of souls will be brought into the kingdom. These two events cannot happen apart from the grace of God. There is great need today for a strong vibrant priesthood!

We require a fresh appreciation of how much we need His grace in the days that face us. Peter expresses it this way:

> *Therefore, gird up your minds for action, keep sober in spirit, fix your hope* ***completely*** *on the grace to be brought to you at the revelation of Jesus Christ. (1 Peter 1:13)*

What Lies Ahead?

What do I anticipate will mark the coming, great, end-time revival? I believe that it will be greater than anything ever experienced by the church. Deep darkness will cover the earth, but the glory of God will rise upon the church everywhere to draw people to Himself from all nations (Haggai 2:6-9). I don't believe this revival will be identified by a man or even a nation; all will know that the Lord Himself is sovereignly responsible for what takes place. The church will be marked by both unity and glory!

The purpose of God is the burden of the Lord. Our call as priests is to share that burden in prayer and worship, and to make His heart known to the church. I believe the Lord will raise up a "faceless generation" of priests who will not build personal kingdoms of ministry. They will be committed to prayer, not simply to pray for the Lord to move as He has in past revivals, but to move according to the burden on His heart for the last days. It will be a time of great harvest!

Chapter 7

Spiritual Warfare

The Battleground

The place where battles are fought is important. Pilots in an Airforce are equipped to fight in the air; sailors are trained for warfare on water and the infantry is trained for combat on land.

Under our Commander-in-Chief, Jesus Christ, we who belong to Him are at war against a hierarchical spiritual realm of evil. Because we are tripartite in our being, body, soul and spirit, it is vital that we fully understand where battles will be fought. Although Satan attacks each part of our being there is one crucial part of our soul that he seeks to control. This is where the most important battle will be fought. Consider the words of Paul:

> *For though we walk in the flesh, we do not war according to the flesh, for the weapons of our warfare are not of the flesh, but divinely powerful for the destruction of fortresses.* ***We are destroying speculations (reasonings) and every lofty thing raised up against the knowledge of God, and we are taking every thought captive to the obedience of Christ.*** *(2 Corinthians 10:3-5)*

This battleground is our mind and will. It comes down to first recognizing that human reasoning and ways of thinking will lead to disobeying Christ. When one's mind-set is contrary to the will of God it is a fortress that must be destroyed, since it is a vulnerable door of access to Satan. Some common fortresses are:

pride, unforgiveness, fantasies, racism, lust, pornography, bigotry, elitism, intolerance and the desire to manipulate and control others.

Only when we are submitted to the will of Christ can we walk in victory and be able to deliver others from the forces of evil.

> *Submit therefore to God. Resist the devil and he will flee from you. (James 4:7)*

The greatest obstacle to victory is not the power of Satan; it is our own ego or self-centered will. This is why the Lord commands us to be transformed by the renewing of our mind; a renewal that enables us to know the will of God.

> *And do not be conformed to this world, but be transformed by the* ***renewing of your mind,*** *so that you may prove what the will of God is, that which is good and acceptable and perfect. (Romans 12:2)*

If we practice sin, we give Satan a legal right to attack our being. When we are submitted to Christ and put on His righteousness, we will walk in His victory over Satan.

Thus, the most important battle we will ever fight against evil is to humble ourselves and submit our mind and will to the will of Christ. Then, by faith, to walk in the glorious victory that He has purchased for us on the cross!

Keys of the Kingdom

> *I will give you the keys of the kingdom of heaven; and whatever you shall bind on earth shall have*

been bound in heaven, and whatever you shall loose on earth shall have been loosed in heaven. (Matthew 16:19)

Two keys are necessary for successful ministry in the Spirit against the forces of evil. They are an essential part of the gospel of the kingdom. The keys are the *power* and the *authority* of God, identified by the Greek words DUNAMIS and EXOUSIA respectively. Each key is uniquely related to one part of our inner man as illustrated in Figure 9.

A policeman's badge and uniform signify his authority, while his gun constitutes his power. Governments in the world operate and maintain order through power and authority. And so does the kingdom of God!

The power of God is resident in the Holy Spirit. He is the "key of power" that we believers receive when He comes to dwell in our spirits.

But you will receive power when the Holy Spirit has come upon you . . . . (Acts 1:8)

With this key we can proclaim the word of God with power, loose the bonds of wickedness and break yokes of oppression. Greater is He who is in us than he who is in the world! This key is limited if we believe that we can accomplish things in our own strength, but it is *perfected* when we recognize our own human weaknesses (2 Corinthians 12:9-10).

The authority of God is resident in the Person and name of the Lord Jesus Christ.

. . . All authority has been given to Me in heaven and on earth. (Matthew 28:18)

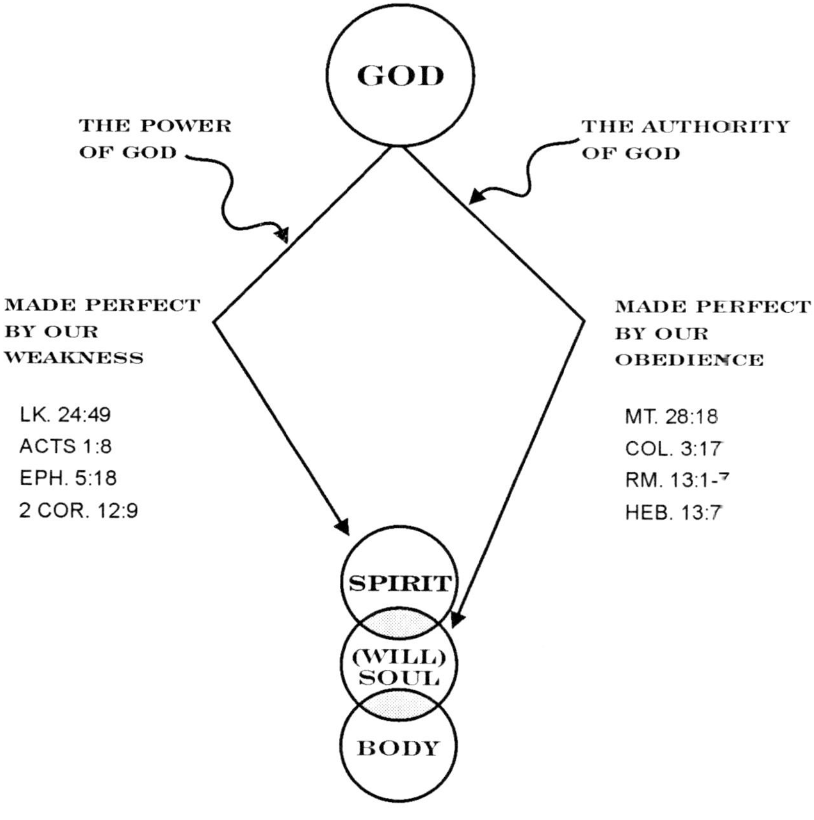

KEYS OF THE KINGDOM

FIGURE 9

Whatever you do in word or deed, do all in the name of the Lord Jesus, giving thanks through Him to God the Father. (Colossians 3:17)

The authority by which the church executes all ministry functions, such as proclamations, ordinations, casting out demons, baptizing believers, etc., is resident in the name of the Lord Jesus Christ.

As we consciously bend our wills in submission to Him, we are given authority according to the purpose and call of God on our lives. *Just as the power of God is made perfect by our weaknesses, so the key of authority is made perfect by our submission and obedience to Him.*

Preaching the gospel, ministry in spiritual warfare, and all other forms of ministry will not be fruitful apart from both keys. Many believers who have been baptized in the Holy Spirit do not experience the results that they expected. The reason may not be a lack of faith, but a lack of submission to God-given authority. If we are truly submitted to God we will not act as "lone-rangers," for we must walk in submission to *all* authority that God has established. This includes appropriate, accountable submission in the body of Christ, and subjection to governmental authority (Ephesians 5:21; 1 Peter 2:13-18).

Every person is to be in subjection to the governing authorities. For there is no authority except from God, and those which exist are established by God. (Romans 13:1)

The gospel of the kingdom offers the following keys to all who will respond in repentance and faith:

- Accept the work of My cross; submit to My authority and allow Me to rule your life.
- Be filled with My Spirit for power to serve and to become like Me.

Knowing the Adversary

Our warfare is not against evil people; it is against spiritual forces of wickedness, both in heavenly places and on earth. Because our adversary is spiritual, we must be strong in the Lord's power.

> *Finally,* ***be strong in the Lord*** *and in the strength of His might. Put on the full armor of God that you will be able to stand against the schemes of the devil. For our struggle is not against flesh and blood, but against the* ***rulers,*** *against the* ***authorities,*** *against the* ***world forces of this darkness, against the spiritual forces of wickedness in the heavenly*** *places. Therefore, take up the full armor of God, so that you will be able to resist in the evil day, and having done everything, to stand firm. (Ephesians 6:10-13)*

Spiritual warfare takes place in two realms; first, against the earthly or world forces of evil manifested by the demonic control of unregenerate men, and secondly, against wicked rulers and authorities in the heavens who give direction to the demonic forces on earth.

These hierarchical forces of evil are Satan's kingdom of darkness. Figure 10 illustrates some of his spiritual attacks against the body, soul and spirit of men.

Because the rulers and authorities are important in Satan's strategy of evil, it is necessary to learn what the word of God says about them. The following are some observations of the spiritual forces of wickedness in heavenly places.

1. These spirit beings are fallen angels who were originally created by God for His purposes, but who followed Satan in his rebellion.

   For by Him all things were created, both in the heavens and on earth, visible and invisible, whether thrones or dominions or ***rulers or authorities*** *. . . . (Colossians 1:16)*

2. In his strategy of evil, Satan has placed certain fallen angels as his representative over nations, regions and localities (Daniel 10:13, 20). Scripture refers to these fallen angelic majesties as principalities (or rulers) and authorities. They have also been referred to as territorial spirits in recent years.

3. Through His death on the cross, and His resurrection, Jesus triumphed over Satan. All angels, authorities and powers were subjected to Him (1 Peter 3:22). In doing so, He also *disarmed* (stripped) the rulers and authorities. However, He did not remove them from their place in the heavens.

   When He had disarmed the rulers and authorities, He made a public display of them having triumphed over them . . . . (Colossians 2:15)

   These angelic beings are now powerless to touch believers except through their control of demonic forces of wickedness on the earth. Here they seek

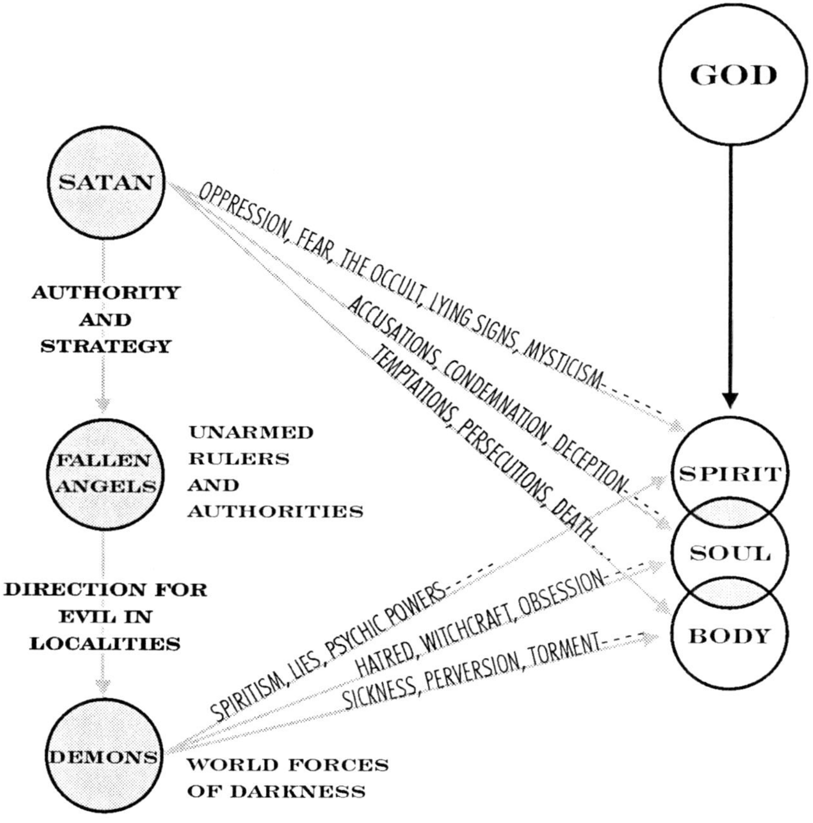

OUR ADVERSARY

FIGURE 10

to accentuate specific expressions of evil in each locality by multiplying current acts of lawlessness, or by building on grievous sins from the past that were not repented of, or for which forgiveness was never extended.

While it is important to know our adversary and to understand his schemes, our victory comes from knowing the Lord and emphasizing His Person, power and purpose! Our emphasis is *never* to be Satan!

Our Weapons of Warfare

The weapons and resources available for believers to wage spiritual warfare are illustrated in Figure 11. The greatest of these ten is the victory of Christ on the cross. God's angels are His weapons and our allies.

I can do all things through Him who strengthens me! (Philippians 4:13)

Great promises of eternal rewards are made for those who overcome; and we can overcome if we are strong in the Lord and the power of His might. The place to start overcoming is within ourselves. It is unfortunate that some believers relate overcoming only to doing battle with Satan, such as casting out demons, etc. Such activities are indeed spiritual warfare, but they are not our first priority.

In warfare, it is not attacking the enemy that comes first, but being trained and prepared for warfare. To successfully defeat Satan, we must, first, be able to stand firm against his attacks. All defensive armor should be in place before one seizes the sword of the Spirit and goes on the attack (Ephesians 6:10-18). The order in which we are commanded to arm ourselves illustrates this truth:

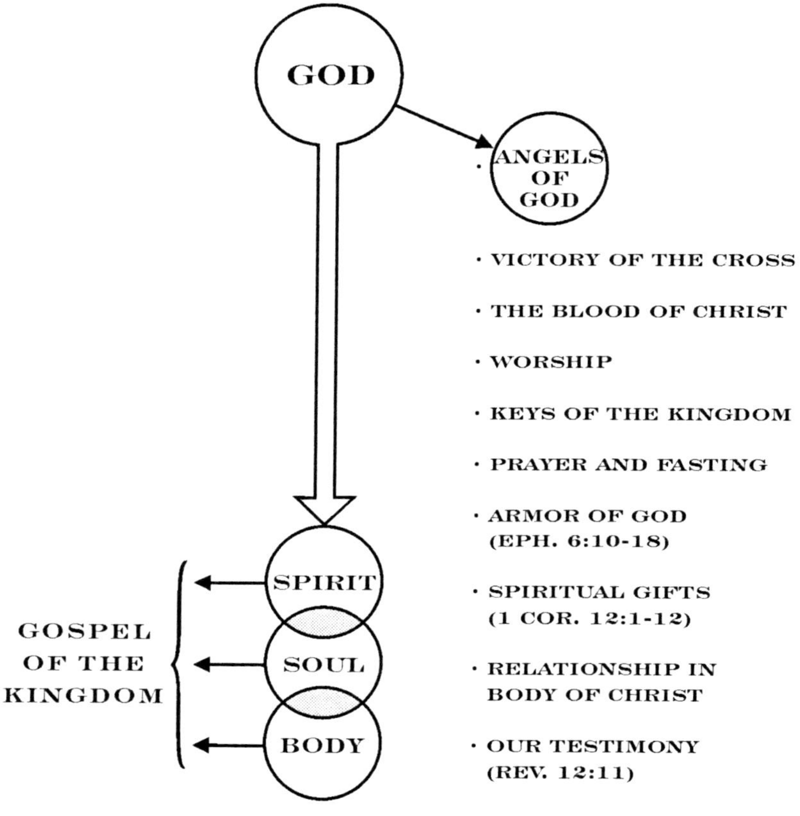

OUR WEAPONS OF WARFARE

FIGURE 11

1. *Girding our loins with truth*
   The loins represent our most vulnerable area, consisting of the abdomen and the generative organs. To gird, or cover, this area is to be established in all truth related to spiritual nourishment and reproduction in the kingdom.

2. *Breastplate of righteousness*
   This covers the heart, and is therefore most important: one will not be an effective warrior unless his heart is free from all unrighteousness, such as envy, pride, deceit, guile, bitterness, unbelief, wrong motives, etc. Satan can recognize such sins and condemn us through his accusations. We must give him no such place, for he would put us in a prison of introspection.

3. *Feed shod with the preparation (readiness) of the gospel of peace*
   We are to be always ready to proclaim the gospel of the kingdom, and to bring the peace of His government into lives.

4. *The shield of faith*
   This piece of armor can be moved around to protect one from attacks of the devil which may come from any direction. To take the shield of faith means to have complete faith in what the word of God declares concerning:
   —Himself
   —Myself
   —My circumstances
   —My brothers in Christ
   These are the directions from which Satan attacks us.

5. *The helmet of salvation*
The helmet speaks of the mind of Christ which we have through the renewal of our minds. We have been accepted in the beloved and there is no place for rejection, depression, despair or discouragement. We are not to move on the basis of logic or reason, but in submission to the revealed will of God.

Having put on all of the armor that protects us, we find there is none for the rear. This tells us we must always *face* Satan; we are *not to fear him* and run from him, nor are we to ignore him. With these five pieces of armor on, we can then take up the sword of the Spirit and be confident of victory. Once these six pieces of armor are in place, the next verse of scripture identifies the very heart of warfare dynamics.

> *With **all** prayer and petition pray at **all** times in the Spirit and with this in view, be on the alert with **all** perseverance and petition for **all** the saints. (Ephesians 6:18)*

God's Strategy for Warfare

The Lord's strategy for spiritual warfare addresses all parts of Satan's kingdom.

His strategy against the world forces of darkness is simple and straight forward. We are to proclaim and manifest the love of God as we preach the gospel of the kingdom with signs and wonders. It is vital to control the battlefield of our mind. We are not to harbor unrighteous thoughts, imaginations or fantasies. Our mind is to focus on hearing and obeying the Lord. We must avoid any meditation where we remove all thoughts and blank out our minds. This can open the door to Satan. When demons are encountered, they are to be "cast out." They are not to be feared nor are they to be reasoned with; they must be cast out of all people who seek to be free of them. A person who has had demons cast out must understand their commitment to Christ is to be total, without reservation. Otherwise the demons can return.

The issue in warfare against spiritual forces of wickedness in heavenly places is primarily one of government; either the government of God's kingdom or the lawlessness of Satan. Divine strategy is to displace and replace Satan's spiritual "covering" of evil over cities, regions and nations with the government of the Lord Jesus Christ, and thereby open the door for a great harvest of souls.

Whenever believers fail to walk in righteousness, they extend a legal right for demonic forces of evil to harass them. If there is disunity, backbiting, gossip or other secret sins.in the church, such as pornography, adultery, witchcraft, etc. the church will be crippled and powerless against the demonic forces which feed on the sins. The principalities of evil in the heavens will seek to amplify such evil over that area and to extend it to other regions, including the nation. The spirit of Allah and Islamic terrorism is one example; the influence of witchcraft in America by the spirit of Jezebel is another example.

There are three clear strategic actions that should be taken for successful warfare.

1. Be concerned first for our own life, our church and our locality. Repent and forsake all sin; walk in righteousness before God. In essence, starve all demonic activity. Preach the gospel, heal the sick and cast out demons.

2. Discern the identity and nature of Satan's spiritual authorities over the area. The history of the region should be studied in order to identify significant events of evil in the past, such as acts of war, murders, massacres, racism, slavery, occult activities, etc. These may have given rise to specific demonic activities. Such an examination could lead to a conviction of the need to repent, to seek forgiveness or group reconciliation so that revival can come.

3. The churches of the area are to unite in proclaiming the gospel, in standing together against false ministries and in praying against the spiritual authority of evil over the area. By presenting a united, godly, spiritual covering for the locality, the church can, in time, displace and replace the authority that Satan had put over the area. *Only Jesus can bring this to pass!* It will not happen apart from a sincere commitment by God's people to stand united in united prayer and intercession. This is the essence of our struggle against rulers and authorities. It is useless and presumptive for believers to attempt to cast down principalities and authorities over their geographic area. We are to bind and cast out demons, but only the Lord can deal with these fallen, angelic majesties in the heavens. We are to unite in prayer against them, but the issue is authority. We believers are to unite in our submission to Him, so that He truly rules over our personal and church lives. He must be allowed to establish His authority over the area as head of the church. He will then displace the authority that

Satan has placed over the area. This is the key to His glory rising upon His people to bring in the great end-time harvest.

In the beginning God gave Adam stewardship of the earth. By his fall into sin, Adam lost this position of authority to Satan, who became the god of this world.

At Calvary, Jesus began the work of restoring redeemed mankind to the glory and oversight that was lost. All of creation eagerly awaits this restoration and revelation of God's sons.

> *For the anxious longing of the creation waits eagerly for the revealing of God's sons . . . . that the creation itself also will be set free from its slavery to corruption into the freedom of the glory of the children of God. For we know that the whole creation groans and suffers the pains of childbirth together until now. (Romans 8:19, 21, 22)*

This is a task that will be completed by the Lord Jesus Christ working through His body. Until the lordship of Christ is fully established over His people in the church, it will not be established in the earth. This is the heart of God's eternal purpose which He is carrying out in the Lord Jesus. *The essence of His strategy is the displacing of rulers and authorities over geographic areas of the earth until finally, there arises unique warfare that involves Michael, the archangel, that will displace Satan from his place in the heavens (Revelation 12:7-12)*. Jesus will then return to establish His kingdom on earth.

In His wisdom, God has determined to reveal His will and government to the rulers and authorities through those in the church who will lay down their personal wills and humble themselves to His lordship.

Through wholehearted submission and obedience to Christ, they will demonstrate to rulers and authorities the Lord's reign over their geographic locality. As they preach the gospel in power, and stand united in prayer against the ruler and authority over their locality, a wonderful change will take place! New godly oversight will begin to replace the evil influence over the region; because of the new manifested presence of God, there will be a great harvest of souls.

> *. . . to bring to light what is the administration (stewardship) of the mystery which for ages has been hidden in God, who created all things; so that **the manifold wisdom of God might now be made known through the church to the rulers and authorities in the heavenly places. This was in accordance with the eternal purpose** which He carried out in Christ Jesus our Lord. (Ephesians 3:9-11)*

This transition to righteousness will involve shakings in the heavens and great warfare against the darkness of evil in regions and nations. There will be deep darkness in the world, but the glory of God will rise upon His people to bring in a final ingathering of souls.

> *Arise, shine; for you light has come, and the **glory of the Lord has risen upon you. For behold, darkness will cover the earth and deep darkness the peoples; but the Lord will rise upon you and His glory will appear upon you. Nations will come to your light,** and kings to the brightness of your rising. (Isaiah 60:1-3)*

This is His strategy for warfare!

The Goal

Having the correct strategy is certainly a key to a successful campaign in warfare. The Christian's goal is simple but vital: the battle has already been won; our part is to enter into the victory that is ours and take the spoils. We are to overcome the world, the flesh and the devil.

Jesus completely triumphed over Satan at Calvary. He reigns now at the right hand of His Father waiting for His enemies to be made His footstool. The word of the Lord states that all things are intended, in time, to come under the feet of man (i.e. the overcomers). Our part, therefore, is to ensure that our lives, motives and actions are always under the Lord's government, for He is the head of the church and commander of His army. Only if we are under His authority today, will we in the future be placed over the works of His hand. His peace within us and among us comes as a result of His government over us. Thus, His headship in our lives is always the first priority in warfare for it is the God of peace who gives us victory over Satan.

If the only purpose of God was to destroy the works of the devil, then Satan and his demons would have been bound at the Lord's resurrection, for he was totally defeated at that time. However, the Lord's plan for His people is that we also, through the power of God, overcome Satan.

Whenever the Lord plants His church in a new locality, there will be a strong man of the enemy over that place who must be confronted. Local expressions of the body of Christ will only be successfully established when His ministers operate in unity under the headship of Christ.

We are to recover what our father Adam lost, namely authority to rule the earth. We are to enter into our Lord's victory, and as workers together with Him, regain the place of authority given to Adam. The Lord will, indeed, finally destroy the works of Satan using His many-membered body as a mighty army. Thus, our goal is to become overcomers in Christ. This is our commission: to resist Satan, to loose from his control those who are appointed for life, and to walk together with all saints under the headship of Christ. We are able to do this being more than conquerors in Christ; we are strong in the power of His might. Praise the Lord!

CHAPTER 8

Christian Fellowship

The Purpose of Fellowship

A personal relationship with the Lord Jesus is always our first priority. However, the purpose of God for our life cannot be accomplished apart from our relationship to one another, a relationship that is based on a common sharing of the life of Christ. This horizontal dimension of salvation has been neglected and underdeveloped in traditional Christianity. Fellowship is the process of building friendship, trust and an accountable commitment between believers so each one can function and grow in his unique place in the body of Christ. It is hindered by jealousy, pride, competition, gossip, tradition, or any other divisive attitude that separates believers. The tradition that divided Christians into two classes—clergy and laity—is one such example. This interpersonal, dependent relationship between believers is described in the scriptures as "joints and ligaments" in order to help us understand the Lord's body from the operation of our own bodies. It is not what I or my brother can do individually that is important, but how we glorify God by *working together as one.*

> *. . . holding fast to the head, from whom the entire body,* ***being supplied and held together by the joints and ligaments,*** *grows with a growth which is from God. (Colossians 2:19)*

> *. . . we are to grow up in all aspects into Him . . . from whom the whole body,* ***being fitted and held together by that which every joint supplies*** *. . . causes the growth of the body for the building up of itself in love. (Ephesians 4:15-16)*

The Process of Fellowship

Figure 12 illustrates the three modes by which we relate to other people. Relationship can be on the basis of physical likeness, such as age, sex, race, etc. Relationship may also be on the basis of a common understanding; that is, unity in knowledge or how something is perceived or defined in our minds. This is the realm where agreement is made on doctrine. Unity on "a least common denominator of belief" is the thrust of ecumenism. When people relate on the basis of what is common among them, and this commonality is limited to the body or soul realms, such groups are cultural and social in nature; they *do not* constitute a valid church.

The church is based on *koinonia* which is fellowship (or communion) in the spirit realm. This only exists when participants are united by the Holy Spirit with Christ. He is the one and only basis of fellowship. When we are individually united with Him in fellowship, we are offered fellowship with all others who are in a similar union with Christ. This defines the body of Christ.

> *What we have seen and heard we proclaim to you also, that you also may have fellowship with us; and indeed our fellowship* ***is with the Father, and with His Son Jesus Christ.*** *(1 John 1:3)*

> *God is faithful, through whom you were called* ***into fellowship with His Son, Jesus Christ our Lord.*** *Now I exhort you, brethren, by the name of our Lord Jesus Christ, that you all agree, and there be no divisions among you . . . . (1 Corinthians 1:9-10)*

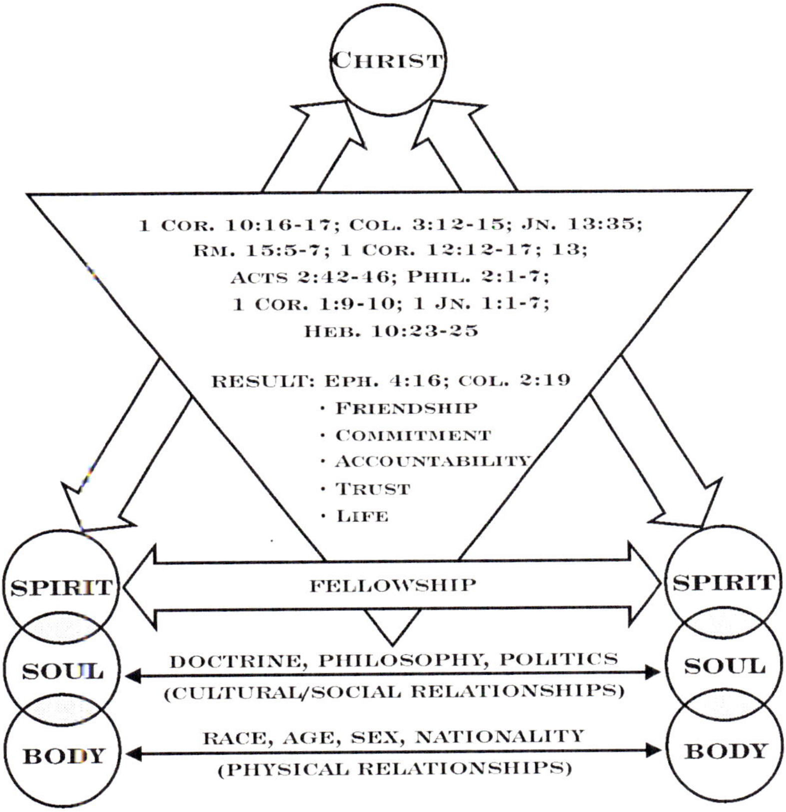

FELLOWSHIP

FIGURE 12

Soulish bonds of relationship tend to be rigid and inflexible. In contrast, spiritual fellowship of mature believers provides an elastic fabric of organic life where an acceptance of one another covers the various personality traits and other differences. How well we walk together marks our maturity in the Spirit.

We are participants in an everlasting covenant with the Lord. This covenant is not just mental assent to certain creeds. We, and all we possess, belong to Christ; and we, in turn, have an inheritance in Him and the glory of His kingdom. Just as Abraham did not hold back Isaac, and God did not hold back His Son, so we cannot hold back anything. It is more than, "Believe in the Lord Jesus Christ"; it requires commitment of our total lives to Him. Fellowship is the experiential walking out of our faith in a family covenant relationship with other believers in Christ. Christians require no other covenant. All agreements and commitments to one another should be based on the new covenant of His blood.

> *If therefore there is any encouragement in Christ, if there is any consolation of* ***love, if there is any fellowship of the Spirit,*** *if any affection and compassion, make my joy complete by being of the* ***same mind, maintaining the same love, united in Spirit, intent on one purpose.*** *Do nothing from selfishness or empty conceit, but with humility of mind let each of you regard one another as more important than himself; do not merely look out for your own personal interests, but also for the interests of others. (Philippians 2:1-4)*

There are two levels of fellowship. first, faith in Christ leads us to a brother/sister relationship with *all* believers. There is a spontaneous response in our hearts whenever we meet a child of God; whomever the Lord has accepted, we must also accept in fellowship. We are one family in Christ.

The second level of fellowship is deeper and is a function of geography. We become committed to a local church, and within that immediate family, we become more deeply related to a smaller number of believers. Stronger bonds of fellowship are built here, for in the informal atmosphere of small meetings, personal idiosyncrasies and facades that each of us have will become apparent and can be healed. We learn to be honest with those who love us, and to develop intimate friendships. A spirit of trust develops, and we become comfortable in being open to others about the less lovely areas of our personal lives. If we don't become honest with one another, we will not be honest with God. It is an atmosphere where each believer can find and fulfill their place of service.

In time, a willingness to be vulnerable and open to correction becomes an important commitment in the covenant we have embraced. This covenant is more than sharing material things; it becomes the sharing of our total lives.

The boards used to construct the tabernacle walls were made from trees of gnarled wood (Exodus 26). Each board, which measured fifteen feet by twenty-seven inches, required a great deal of cutting and trimming so it would form a perfectly true and straight wall. It is the same with us, our human nature is hard, set in its way, twisted from the influence of sin and from going our own way. There is a special place in the wall for which each of us is trimmed and fitted, so that the body of Christ may be complete. Therefore, we *must* know the boards that are next to us; those whom God would relate us to and build us together with. This redemptive work of building relationships is the process that takes place in fellowship.

This process has a threefold result in the hearts of participants.

1. Members become *fitted together* (Ephesians 4:16). This requires the "sandpapering" and "trimming away" of undesirable character traits, something that does not take place overnight.

2. Members are *held together* (Ephesians 4:16; Colossians 2:19). This flows out of the trust and commitment that is built between hearts in the love of God.

3. Members are *supplied* (Colossians 2:19). Once trust and acceptance are established between hearts, there will be an openness to receive the supply of life in ministry from one another.

The ministry gifts, described in chapters 12 and 14 of Paul's first epistle to Corinth, will only be fruitful if they are undergirded by the love of God, described in chapter 13, which is the proper relationship in which to give and receive ministry. Thus, fellowship in the love of God is the environment for ministry in the body of Christ.

Building Fellowship

Those who lay foundations for new churches, who oversee assemblies and equip the saints, must know how to build so as to develop the qualities of spiritual fellowship. This requires recognizing the importance of small groups. Interpersonal relationships where "as iron sharpens iron, so one man sharpens another" will not occur in large central meetings. The interaction necessary to develop character and build bonds of covenant requires fellowship structures of small groups. To be effective these must be under proper oversight of men who are committed to the headship of Christ.

The place to begin is simply learning to accept one another just as Christ has received us.

> *Wherefore, accept one another, just as Christ also accepted us to the glory of God. (Romans 15:7)*

No assembly can be a fully functioning body until every member appreciates his need for all others, and in addition, recognizes the value of his own unique ministry and contribution. Each of us is called to fill a special place in the body of Christ. In our walk with the Lord, each of us wear a pair of custom-made shoes that will fit no one else!

> *If the foot should say, "Because I am not a hand, I am not a part of the body," it is not for this reason any less a part of the body. And if the ear should say, "Because I am not an eye, I am not a part of the body," it is not for this reason any the less a part of the body . . . . But now God has placed the* ***members, each one of them,*** *in the body just as He desired . . . . And the eye cannot say to the hand, "I have no need of you"; or again the head to the feet, "I have no need of you." (1 Corinthians 12:15, 16, 18, 21)*

How does one go about building such virtues in a house church? A primary object lesson should come from observing those who are overseers, if they are leaders who serve, who do not drive or dominate others, but who set an example in humility. When leaders are mutually submitted to one another in sharing the responsibility of oversight, their humility is a demonstration to the saints of how they are to serve each other. Humility and submission will absorb the sharpness of criticism and complaints. Leaders require much grace and gentleness, especially when there is ignorance and opposition (2 Timothy 2:24-25). God saw that the meekness of Moses would enable him to become a great leader.

A biblical way to evangelize and grow the church is through the planting of house churches. After a number of house churches have been established in a locality, joint, central gatherings should not replace or hinder the role of house fellowships. The following are some practical objectives that help ensure the health and success of home meetings:

1. The primary purpose of the home is to be an informal outreach for Christ in that neighborhood.

2. Any teaching should be simple, always pointing people to Christ. Meetings should *not* be miniature versions of the large gatherings.

3. The members should consist of a cross section of family and assembly life. There should not be home meetings for singles, for sisters, for the elderly, etc. The integration of each dimension of family life is required to build a strong church. Each believer should be encouraged to share.

4. A home church should be allowed to develop any unique flow of life which the Lord brings forth in that group. Just as we are different as individuals,

so also there will be diversity in the cell groups in how they desire to express the Lord's life in the community. Individual groups may have a different ministry emphasis, such as hospital visitation, street evangelism, intercessory prayer, music, outreach to the poor, etc.

5. No cliques should be allowed to form. Competitiveness or exclusivity in hearts must be guarded against.

6. Social, recreational and secular activities should be encouraged. Some examples are: eating together, helping others, meeting personal needs (such as repairing a car, painting a house, caring for children, sharing material things, etc.) campouts, retreats, joint ventures in growing food, etc. Such activities are not only good outreach opportunities, but they also help build strong spiritual relationships; the common denominator in each case is sharing the life of Christ.

7. Home churches lose their effectiveness when they become too large in size. Dividing, when a second suitable home and leadership is available, is how the church can grow.

8. The centrality of Christ is the emphasis of all ministry. Thus, two important components in each meeting format are prayer and worship. When these are missing, there is loss of vision and the meeting can become simply a social gathering.

9. A key ministry objective in meetings is to encourage one another in our growth and walk in Christ (Hebrews 10:24-25).

10. Those won to Christ are to be baptized and taught how to share their faith with others. Small groups are where new believers can begin to exercise spiritual gifts. It is much easier to begin such ministry in an informal environment. It is a good place to practice.

11. There can be good reasons why a participant, or family, may want to change home groups. However, it should not be for the reason of running from a problem. Victory comes when we learn to embrace our problems where we are. The conflicts that do arise, often serve to develop hearts of peacemakers in others, especially the leaders. Therefore, times of stress are a normal part of the growth process.

12. Finally, it must be made clear to participants the importance of building character and relationship. A valid, lasting strength in spiritual relationships between believers is work of the Holy Spirit. It is character derived from the fruits of the Spirit, not from agreement on doctrine, that bonds us together in the body of Christ. The virtues related to unity in the following verses make this abundantly clear.

*I therefore, the prisoner of the Lord, entreat you to walk in a manner worthy of the calling with which you have been called, with all **humility and gentleness, with patience, showing forbearance to one another in love**, being diligent to preserve the **unity of the Spirit in the bond of peace.** (Ephesians 4:1-3)*

*And so, as those who have been chosen of God, holy and beloved, put on a heart of **compassion, kindness, humility, gentleness and patience; bearing with one another, and forgiving** each*

> *other, whoever has a complaint against anyone, just as the Lord forgave you,* ***so also should you. And beyond all these things put on love, which is the perfect bond of unity.*** *(Colossians 3:12-14)*

The character virtues in these verses define the quality of spiritual fellowship. Thus:

> *If we walk in the light as He Himself is in the light, we have fellowship with one another, and the blood of Jesus His Son cleanses us from all sin. (1 John 1:7)*

Hatred, gossip, strife and backbiting, if not dealt with promptly, can destroy fellowship and fracture a church.

The Sacrament of Fellowship

> *Is not the cup of blessing which we bless a* ***sharing*** *in the blood of Christ? Is not the bread which we break a* ***sharing*** *in the body of Christ? Since there is one bread, we who are many are* ***one body; for we all partake of one bread.*** *(1 Corinthians 10:16-17)*

Communion is the sacrament which expresses and proclaims the covenant we have embraced with Christ. This we are to celebrate frequently. It is not like baptism which is a one-time experience.

Each communion service is a proclamation of the covenant for it points us back to the death of the Lord Jesus. As we share together in His body, which was broken for us, we reaffirm our commitment to be one spiritual body united in Him. To participate requires that we first reexamine the integrity of our own heart.

If we are deficient in any way (such as possessing animosity toward a brother, or if unrepented sin exists in our life, etc.), these things must first be dealt with before we eat and drink.

If we do not discern the body of Christ correctly, that is, if we fail to see the importance of our relationship to others, and we eat and drink without making things right, we can sin to the point of death. However, if we truly discern the Lord's body, we will not cause division nor introduce the leaven of sin. For this reason, examining ourselves is a mandatory and vital part of communion. Once we grasp the importance of communion in fellowship and covenant life, it will be much more real to us. Communion may be celebrated in the family circle, in the home church, as well as in the assembly since each one of these settings is an expression of covenant life.

> *Behold, how good and how pleasant it is for brothers to dwell together in unity! It is like the precious oil upon the head, coming down upon the beard, even Aaron's beard, coming down upon the edge of his robes. It is like the dew of Hermon, coming down upon the mountains of Zion;* ***for there the Lord commanded the blessing—life forever.*** *(Psalm 133)*

Fellowship expresses the unity of our common life in Christ; ministry is the dynamics of sharing that life.

CHAPTER 9

MINISTRY

The Principle of Ministry

The Greek word DIAKONOS is translated as minister or servant. To minister is to serve others.

Spiritual ministry does not consist only of actions and words, it is an impartation of life, where truth is communicated or demonstrated from one person to another. Godly character comes from the presence of Christ in our spirit, and it is from here that motivation and unction for ministry arises. What takes place in those who receive ministry may occur in their body, spirit or soul, but it *must* have its origin in the Spirit of Christ if life is to result. Ministry is not a sovereign act by the Holy Spirit; it requires obedient faith by the one whose spirit-senses have been anointed to minister what has been quickened to him. The intended recipient also requires faith and a hunger to receive what is being offered to him.

Satan can counterfeit gifts of the Holy Spirit; therefore, we dare not accept ministry only on the basis of supernatural demonstrations. True ministry will produce righteousness, exalt the Lord Jesus and bring His purposes to pass in lives. This will *never* be counterfeited by Satan.

Similar to fellowship, ministry can occur at three different levels as illustrated in Figure 13. Ministry in the body realm can take the form of sharing material things such as food, shelter, clothing or even a glass of cold water. Such acts of ministry are not insignificant, they are a vital part of Christian life when given in the

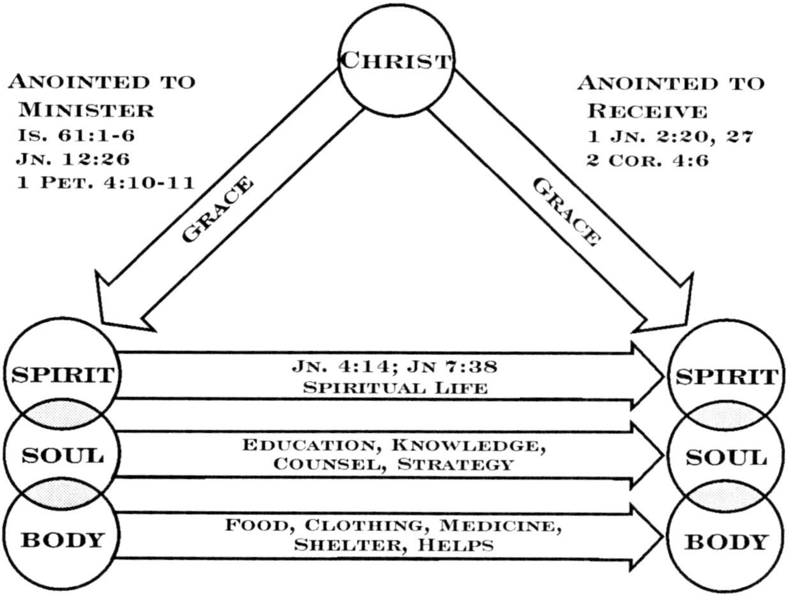

CATEGORIES OF MINISTRY

- <u>ASCENSION GIFT MINISTRIES</u>:

  EPH. 2:19-22; 4:11-16; 1 COR. 14:29-32; ACTS 13:1-3
- <u>SPIRITUAL GIFTS</u>:

  1 COR. 12:1-27; 14, RM. 12:1-8
- <u>MINISTRIES OF RELATIONSHIP</u>:

  RM. 12:9-18 GAL. 6:1-2; 1 COR. 13:4-7; COL. 3:12-16; HEB. 10:23-25; 12:12-15; 1 THESS. 5:11-15

MINISTRY

FIGURE 13

spirit of love and compassion. We are taught of God to share our worldly goods with one another when such needs arise in the assembly (James 2:15-16). If we are not first committed to this level of service, we will have very little else to offer in ministry.

Another dimension of ministry is the impartation of knowledge and instruction at the soul level. This educational process serves to develop wisdom and understanding in recipients' minds and soundness in their emotions.

Facts, concepts, principles, associations and information, when imparted to children's minds over time, help to develop adult mentalities. Education depends on communication, and it is greatly reinforced through observing how truth is practiced by others, especially those who do the teaching, Our life is a book read by those around us. What we say and how we act conditions the knowledge and influence that others receive from us. This is why godly character is so very important. What we are speaks louder than our words.

Truth begins with revealed knowledge. No matter how true it is, knowledge by itself does one little good. Knowledge alone can lead to pride unless the heart of the recipient is conditioned to apply the knowledge toward godliness. This is where the Holy Spirit does His work. God's life flows in the realm of our spirits. If there is no such flow of the Spirit between hearts, even when there is a valid impartation to the soul or body, there will be no spiritual ministry. Evil men can do deeds of kindness, but that is not ministry. Ministry must be anointed by the Holy Spirit if it is to bring life.

> *He who believes in Me, as the Scripture said, "From **his innermost being** will flow rivers of living water." (John 7:38)*

Isaiah 61:1-3 presents a wonderful overview of what exemplifies true spiritual ministry. These are the verses that Jesus used to identify His mission of redemption on earth.

Acts of the Holy Spirit represent a multifaceted diversity that is implicit in the will of God. Although His acts cannot be confined to theological definitions, there appears to be three general classes of spiritual ministry through which the Lord builds His church. The first of these are "ministries of relationship."

Ministries of Relationship

Every believer possesses the Spirit of God, and therefore has a ministry; a place of service in the body of Christ. Ministry is simply the Spirit expressing Himself through the spirit, soul and body of believers. This does not take place by compulsion, but through a willing obedience to promptings or leadings of the Holy Spirit. When the saints gather together in fellowship, there will arise occasions when some will be prompted by the Holy Spirit to reach out and encourage or exhort others. Since such personal interactions develop relationships, I have chosen to call them "ministries of relationship."

There are important guidelines on how believers should assemble in order to facilitate such ministry. For example, the freedom and opportunity for developing relationships is obviously much better in small group environments. This is undoubtedly a reason why the early church met so often in homes. The following are three beneficial characteristics of small groups: simplicity, informality and freedom to share. These provide a non-religious environment where one can learn from mistakes; where practical person-to-person interactions can promote spiritual growth because believers are free to be honest with one another and to remove make-believe facades. It is an atmosphere where accountability can grow. The central focus of meetings should always be the Lord Jesus and seeking to hear His voice.

The following is a list of biblical ministries of relationship. These activities can take place in one-on-one situations or in group meetings.

- Hospitality

  Be hospitable to one another without complaint. (1 Peter 4:9)

  When we come to Christ, we bring not only our hearts but all that we posses, and this includes our home. Being hospitable is how we offer it to Him. Hospitality is essential in building the relational fabric of church life since it so largely depends on family lives that make up the church.

- Making friends

  Be devoted to one another . . . . (Romans 12:10)

  Faithful are the wounds of a friend . . . . (Proverbs 27:6)

  When correction comes from a true friend it is more likely to be received, even though it may hurt at the time.

- Table fellowship

  Breaking bread together in the sharing of meals is an excellent means of building friendships. This was a common practice in the early church, as well as in the ministry of Jesus with His disciples.

- Encouraging others

  Therefore encourage one another, and build up one another . . . . (1 Thessalonians 5:11)

  But encourage one another day after day . . . lest any one of you be hardened by the deceitfulness of sin. (Hebrews 3:13)

- Identifying with the emotions of others

  Rejoice with those who rejoice, and weep with those who weep. (Romans 12:15)

- Comforting the afflicted

  Blessed be . . . the God of all comfort, who comforts us in all our affliction so that we will be able to comfort those who are in any affliction with the comfort with which we ourselves are comforted by God. (2 Corinthians 1:3-4)

  It is in our trials and difficulties that we experience the comfort of God. Through this we learn how to comfort others. We cannot give something that we do not possess. Only if we have experienced the lifting of a heavy burden in our lives by the Lord are we likely to be constrained through compassion to bear the burdens of others.

- Being a peacemaker

  One of the most precious ministries for building relationship is that of a peacemaker. We may think a peacemaker is one who comes between warring parties and stops the fighting. We equate God's peace to an armistice, which is not the case. Peace is not a passive absence of conflict, it is the active government of God in lives. There is peace wherever He reigns. The role of peacemaking is to bring each heart into submission to the Lord, who is the Prince of Peace.

  And the seed whose fruit is righteousness is sown in peace by those who make peace. (James 3:18)

- The ministry of helps

  Helps is not limited to the service of deacons. It expresses how to support one another in the church through one's presence, time or possessions. God has designed us so that we *cannot* make it alone; *we need each other*!

  And the eye cannot say to the hand, "I have no need of you"; or again the head to the feet, "I have no need of you." (1 Corinthians 12:21)

  Helps is how to share in and support the ministry of others, and to nullify the spirit of competition.

The following verses of scripture are specific expressions of body ministry where members build up one another in the life and love of Christ. A key requirement is the group dynamics where there is freedom and opportunity to express and practice these exhortations.

Therefore, ***strengthen the hands that are weak and the knees that are feeble . . . see to it that no one comes short of the grace of God;*** *that no root of bitterness springing up causes trouble, and by it many be defiled. (Hebrews 12:12, 15)*

Be kind to one another, tenderhearted, forgiving each other, *just as God in Christ also has forgiven you. (Ephesians 4:32)*

Let no unwholesome word proceed from your mouth, but only ***such a word as is good for edification*** *according to the need of the moment,* ***that it may give grace to those who hear.*** *(Ephesians 4:29)*

And let us consider how to ***stimulate one another to love and good deeds,*** *not forsaking our own assembling together, as is the habit of some,* ***but encouraging one another*** *. . . . (Hebrews 10:24-25)*

Above all, ***keep fervent in your love for one another,*** *because love covers a multitude of sins. (1 Peter 4:8)*

And so, as those who have been chosen of God, holy and beloved, ***put on a heart of compassion, kindness, humility, gentleness and patience;*** *bearing with one another, and* ***forgiving each other,*** *whoever has a complaint against anyone; just as the Lord forgave you, so also should you.* ***And beyond all these things put on love, which is the perfect bond of unity.*** *Let the peace of Christ rule in your hearts, to which indeed you were called in one body* ***and be thankful. Let the word of Christ richly dwell within you,*** *with all*

> *wisdom* ***teaching and admonishing one another*** *with psalms and hymns and spiritual songs,* ***singing with thankfulness in your hearts to God.*** *(Colossians 3:12-16)*

It is apparent that, while ministries of relationship involve the spirit, soul and body of believers, it is the qualities of godly character in the heart (spirit) that the Holy Spirit uses to impart life and truth to others. To give counsel without such character can be to simply meddle in lives. The following scripture endorses this truth.

> *And concerning you, my brethren, I myself also am convinced that you yourselves are* ***full of goodness, filled with all knowledge and able also to admonish one another.*** *(Romans 15:14)*

Finally, it is good to remember how our words and our conduct will affect those who we are in relationship with.

> *Iron sharpens iron, so one man sharpens another. (Proverbs 27:17)*

The second category of ministry that we will address is that of spiritual gifts.

Gifts of the Holy Spirit

Paul's apostolic writings emphasize the importance of spiritual gifts in the life of the church.

> *For I long to see you* ***that I may impart some spiritual gift to you,*** *that you may be established. (Romans 1:11)*

> *Now concerning spiritual gifts, brethren, I do not want you to be unaware (uninformed). (1 Corinthians 12:1)*

> *Pursue love, yet* ***desire earnestly spiritual gifts,*** *but especially that you may prophesy. (1 Corinthians 14:1)*

In his epistle to Corinth, Paul identifies nine gifts which are distributed to individuals according to the will of the Holy Spirit (1 Corinthians 12:4-11). Although spiritual gifts may be manifested through human faculties, they are initiated by the anointing of the Holy Spirit on one's spiritual senses. Three of these relate to specific manifestations of the power of God: the working of miracles, the gifts of healing, and the gift of faith. Three gifts concern unique operation of the Holy Spirit in the minds of believers: the word of knowledge, the word of wisdom, and the discerning of spirits. The remaining three gifts concern specific operations of the Holy Spirit in vocal utterances: the gift of prophecy, speaking in tongues (unknown languages), and the interpretation of tongues.

Two of the more important tools in pastoral work are the gift of the word of knowledge and the word of wisdom. The gift of the word of knowledge is a supernatural deposit of knowledge by the Spirit through the spiritual sense window of the believer, who then must have faith to recognize and accept it. Such knowledge will be important for some person or situation. It will generally not involve much information, but is a *word* of knowledge, something that is critical to specific needs of a believer or of an assembly at the time. Examples in the New Testament include the story of Ananias and Sapphira (Acts 5:1-5); the Samaritan woman at the well to whom Jesus ministered (John 4:17-18); and the

Lord's instruction to Peter that he would find sufficient money for their taxes in the mouth of a fish (Matthew 17:24-27). When Paul visited Ephesus he knew by the word of knowledge that it would be the last time he would see them (Acts 20:25, 38). He also knew in the Spirit about the division that would later occur among them, and warned them accordingly. A word of knowledge was the reason why Paul knew he would survive the trip to Rome from Crete, but that the ship and cargo would be lost in the storm (Acts 27:10). This particular gift is indispensable in the counseling, overseeing functions of an eldership. It is not related to one's natural knowledge. The spirit of divination is a satanic counterfeit of the word of knowledge.

The word of wisdom has nothing to do with natural wisdom, whether abundant or scarce. It comes to pass when the Lord anoints the mind of a believer through his spiritual senses to impart a word of supernatural wisdom for a situation where natural wisdom is inadequate. Jesus often manifested this gift in His times of confrontation with the religious leaders (Luke 20:21-25; Matthew 21:24-25). A good example of this particular gift is found in the story of the woman who was taken in the act of adultery and brought to Jesus for stoning. To keep the Law, which He was required to do, meant that He had to support the act of stoning. However, He came to reveal the mercy and forgiveness of God. He did not know what to do or to say, for there was no obvious answer. Therefore, He did nothing, but stooped down and wrote on the ground waiting for His Father to give Him direction. The answer came, a perfect word of wisdom:

> *He who is without sin among you, let him be the first to throw a stone at her. (John 8:7)*

The word of wisdom will be exactly correct for a given situation.

How often we answer out of our rational wisdom instead of seeking God for a word of wisdom.

The gift of discerning spirits is similar to the word of knowledge since it involves an impartation of supernatural knowledge concerning the presence and/or identity of an evil spirit in a person (Acts 16:16-17). Neglect of this particular gift can allow Satan to gain access and influence in the church through counterfeit ministry that eventually could divide and hurt the saints. He can come as an angel of light and be accepted by many if this gift is not present. This possibility must be guarded against, especially in the days of conflict that lie ahead (1 Timothy 4:1-3). An individual who accepts Christ without confessing and renouncing any earlier participation in the occult may need deliverance from demons. This gift would reveal such a condition, and prevent the person from introducing confusion into an assembly.

The gifts of utterance are revelatory or prophetic in nature since they are expressions from the heart of God for His people at that time. When accompanied by interpretation, the gift of tongues is essentially equal to the gift of prophecy (1 Corinthians 14:5). The gift of prophecy is to edify, exhort and comfort the church.

God's people are to be a prophetic people in the earth, and these three vocal gifts are a means for this to take place, We will fall short in the church if we build only on traditions of the past. Of course, we are to judge all revelation in the light of the written word, for it is our foundation for accuracy and stability. However, we must know the heart of *God for today*. It is vital to build and move forward on the basis of what God is *currently* speaking to us. We are to hold as precious the truths of our foundation in Him, but we are to walk in the truth that He is revealing today. The past is the foundation upon which we build the present and future. We are living in an exciting era of restoration in the church (Acts 3:21). It is not primarily a matter of major truths, for the Lord desires to speak to us of the little things that hinder our walk with Him. If we require the daily encouragement and exhortation of friends, how much more do we need to hear His words of encouragement and admonition! Prophetic gifts should never take away the preeminent place the scriptures have in our lives; the opposite is true, they should reinforce and endorse the written word. A prophetic people will be a people of His word, a people whose lives and utterances express His word. The more we grow in our knowledge and likeness of Him the more prophetic we will become. Once there exists a fluent prophetic flow in an assembly, it can become very easy to take it for granted. We must frequently remind ourselves of the great honor it is to hear the word of the Lord, and the responsibility we have to obey Him.

> *Do not despise prophetic utterances. But examine everything carefully; hold fast to that which is good (1 Thessalonians 5:20-21)*

The three vocal gifts require an exercise of faith to speak what the Spirit gives us to utter. In the gift of tongues, the speaker's mind is not anointed to understand the sense of what is spoken. The opposite is true in the interpretation of tongues and in prophecy, for the speaker in these instances does understand what he or she is saying. Many may speak in tongues, but not all will have the gift of tongues or of interpretation. Likewise, all believers may have the spirit of prophecy, but not all will have the gift of prophecy (Revelation 19:10; 1 Corinthians 12:10). And fewer yet will be prophets, which is a foundational (or ascension) gift ministry in the church (1 Corinthians 12:28).

The three "power" gifts are frequently demonstrated during the preaching of the gospel to the lost when the Holy Spirit brings an anointing for the supernatural. From the history of the early church it is apparent the Lord placed two emphases in the gospel He has commissioned the church to preach to the nations.

1. First of all, it is a *proclamation* of the good news of salvation; the gospel of His kingdom.

2. Secondly, it is a *demonstration* that what is proclaimed is indeed true, as God works in signs and wonders to prove that Christ was raised from the dead. There is nothing apologetic about the gospel of the kingdom when the sick are healed, demons cast out and lives are transformed. Although we may not see it today, miraculous signs and wonders should be the norm in church life.

The church is to be an expression of the character of God, the words of God and the acts of God. There will only be proper demonstration of His acts in an assembly when all the saints are equipped for service, with each member having a vital and unique part to play in expressing the Lord's life through gifts of His Spirit.

> *For just as we have many members in one body and all members do not have the same function, so we, who are many, are one body in Christ,*

> *and individually members one of another. And since we have gifts that differ according to the grace given to us,* ***let each exercise them accordingly*** *. . . . (Romans 12:4-6)*

The third and last category of ministry to be addressed concerns the five-fold, or ascension gift ministries.

Ascension Gift Ministries

> *And He gave some as* ***apostles****, and some as* ***prophets****, and some as* ***evangelists****, and some as* ***pastors*** *and* ***teachers, for the equipping of the saints for*** *the work of service, to the building up of the body of Christ. (Ephesians 4:11-12)*

The word "equipping" is translated from the Greek word KATARTISMOS which means "to complete," "to prepare" or "train fully." Implicit in this scripture is the truth that a diversity of ministries is required to properly equip the saints; no minister can accomplish this alone.

In addition to ministries of relationship and spiritual gifts, these ministries possess specific grace and anointings with which to equip and disciple believers. They are the Lord's bond-servants representing Him in word and deed by their service and the example of their lives.

The names given to identify these servants of the Lord are not titles, they simply denote ministry functions. It is important to properly recognize the function of such ministries in the way that Christ intends to represent Himself through them. For instance, one does not receive an evangelist as a pastor.

He who receives a prophet in the name of a prophet shall receive a prophet's reward . . . . (Matthew 10:41)

It is important to honor, not the minister, but the grace of God in the ministry; we should not compare one minister with another, but love each one as a servant of the Lord. These principles are how to esteem them in love because of their work. Let us examine the unique grace and gifting of each ministry.

Teachers are necessary to instruct the saints about the Lord and His ways and to equip them to teach, encourage and edify others. A teacher has grace to bring instruction from scriptures in a manner that develops a hunger and appreciation of God's word. Part of the reason is a logic of overall perspective that integrates revelations into concise summary expressions of truth. (The graphic models of this book are such an example.)

Pastors care for the saints, counseling and equipping them by example to love, care for and to admonish others. We are to be our brother's keeper. A pastor has grace to accomplish this because of his love for the people of God. He is able to reveal the heart of God to the saints by his love and commitment to them. Training the people of God with His word involves more than imparting knowledge. It includes counseling that deals with perceptual and behavioral problems where a clear distinction must be made between what is soulish and what is spiritual.

Evangelists impart the Lord's heart of compassion for the lost and equip the saints to evangelize. A church without a vision and strategy for outreach will be a failure. Evangelism is not some technique for delivering a message; it is a witness or presentation of divine life. We are to be witnesses of the life of God. Prayer is an essential component of evangelism.

Prophets have grace to hear and to express the heart of God to individuals, to congregations and even to nations. They play a significant role in the impartation of vision to a church, equipping the saints to be a prophetic people. Prophets bring a greater awareness of the heart and direction of the Lord to His people. Their words endorse the way of righteousness and point to what lies ahead. Without such vision, the saints tend to look back to the past and to traditions of yesterday. The anointing for prophetic insight can come into a prophet's mind, through the window of his spiritual senses, either as words or in a vision. The latter is why prophets in the Old Testament were sometimes called "seers." A prophet will serve to ignite prayer and intercession on issues that are vital to bring God's purpose to fruition in the church. With apostles, they jointly equip, appoint and confirm spiritual gifts and ministries in the saints.

The following are some guidelines for judging personal prophecy; an appraisal where spiritual senses are important.

- The Holy spirit should bear witness with our spirit that it is a word from the Lord.
- The spirit, character and accountability of the prophet should be judged.
- Except for prophetic words that are unconditional, prophecy requires faith and obedience by the recipient to be fulfilled.
- Personal prophecy should exhort, comfort and edify as well as confirm or establish vision and calling. It will occasionally (by a seasoned prophet)

warn or direct about the future. It will always glorify Christ and never contradict the Lord's written word.

- Prophecy will never manipulate or seek to control a person.
- Prophecy usually points to a future fulfillment. One should be cautious of prophecy that sets specific dates.
- Personal prophecy should always be presented under local church oversight; or submitted back to the local church if received from an outside source.

The word, *"apostle,"* means "one sent on a mission." The word is sometimes used by religious bodies to identify a specific position of leadership among them. However, a biblical apostle denotes one whom the Lord Jesus has given to the church with grace and anointing to represent Him in ministry. The first apostles saw themselves representing Christ as His bond-servants. This was the heart of their apostolic calling (James 1:1; 2 Peter 1:1; Revelation 1:1; Jude 1:1).

Paul, a bond-servant of Christ Jesus, called as an apostle . . . . (Romans 1:1)

They sought no self grandeur in title or offices; they were bond-servants of Christ. All five ministries are uniquely a matter of God's grace. There is no difference in greatness or importance between ministries of the Spirit; there is only a difference in grace (Romans 12:6; Ephesians 4:7; 1 Corinthians 15:10). Apostles will have grace to function in one or more of the other four ministries. They also have grace to see the "whole picture" more clearly, and they have a unique grace to lay foundations for the church. Paul describes his apostolic ministry by the word "masterbuilder" (1 Corinthians 3:10). This word is translated from the Greek word ARCHITEKTON from which the English word "architect" is derived. ARCHITEKTON is made up of two root words in Greek, one meaning "to begin" and the other meaning "craftsman." This precisely describes the mission of an apostle; he is one sent by the Lord to lay foundations for local expressions of His body. He will not evangelize and build a following of converts around himself; he will establish them in union with Christ as their Lord and Head. When one lays a foundation upon which to construct a building, the resulting structure will be determined by the intended purpose of the building. A tool shed will not be built like an apartment tower. The purpose defines the structure, which in turn dictates the foundation. A proper foundation must anticipate all that will be built upon it. The Lord has one central purpose for His house; it is to be the place of His presence. It is to become His dwelling place from where He can express the fullness of His glory to all creation! To fulfill this purpose, the foundation *must* be built upon the cornerstone that God has laid for His house, which is Christ Jesus Himself (Isaiah 28:16). This foundation makes Christ central to *all* ministry activity in the church; everything purposed by the Lord flows out of Him as head of the church. He is the builder of the house, the foundation of the house and the head over all things in the house. The church is a spiritual organism; it is *not* a religious institution! Implicit in the foundation will be all the fundamentals of salvation such as, faith, repentance, grace, water baptism, worship, prayer, spiritual gifts and ministries, fellowship, family order, etc. In the end, the importance of all these truths is not the knowledge they represent, but how well they serve to build the saints together into a suitable dwelling place of God through the Spirit.

> *. . . having been built upon the foundation of the apostles and prophets, Christ Jesus Himself being the cornerstone, in whom the whole building, being fitted together is growing into a holy temple in the Lord; in whom you also are being built together into a dwelling of God in the Spirit. (Ephesians 2:19-22)*

The fact that the revelations and teachings of the first generation apostles and prophets have been passed down to us in scripture, does not mean that one can plant "New Testament" churches by simply following a list of biblical procedures, good as they may be. We require the ministry of the Holy Spirit in *all* the gifts and ministries that Christ has given to the church. We must remember that it is He who is building the church! Just as *every* believer needs a personal revelation of truth, so *each* generation of the church requires apostles and prophets, who are anointed by the Holy Spirit with grace and revelation to build local expressions of the body of Christ in their day. An apostle will not wander around as a "lone-ranger." He will be a man sent out by the presbytery of a local church to whom he will be accountable. He will recognize the sphere of his ministry, and he will normally travel with co-workers, which will include some who are being discipled. The pattern for apostolic team ministry is found in Paul's translocal ministry described in chapters 13 to 20 of Acts, and in his epistles to the churches that he established on his travels.

The graphic model of body, soul and spirit can be designed to address additional ministry truths. Four examples are illustrated in the APPENDIX.

CHAPTER 10

I WILL BUILD MY CHURCH

God is a Builder

We who have been redeemed by God's mercy and grace think of Him in many ways; He is our Father, our Lord, our Savior. His power, glory and love for us are beyond our comprehension, and His ways are past finding out. However, there is another significant attribute of God that we don't often think of; He is an architect and builder!

The Bible begins with the creation of man, body, soul and spirit, and it ends with the holy city that God has built for His eternal place of rest, His tabernacle among men. In a sense the Bible is a history of how the building blocks of redeemed men are assembled together by the Holy Spirit to become the dwelling place of God.

The Pattern

God began His covenant relationship with mankind through Abraham, a covenant established on the basis of faith; Abraham believed what God told him concerning His purpose among men. What was this purpose? What was the vision that God built into the heart of Abraham?

> *. . . he (Abraham) was looking for the city which has foundations,* ***whose architect and builder is God****. (Hebrews 11:10)*

God's purpose was centered in a city that He would design and build; a place of His presence and glory.

God gave further revelation of His purpose through Moses. He gave explicit design details to Moses for a tabernacle that he was to build. It would be the place where God dwelt among His people of that day, the nation of Israel. The structure of this tabernacle was a type or shadow of His heavenly sanctuary, and the Lord emphasized that it *must* be built according to the pattern that He gave to Moses (Exodus 25-40). The pattern contained symbolic revelations through the material used, the dimensions and structural details of the walls, the holy place, and the most holy place, all of which pointed toward a future reality. In the same way, every piece of furniture in its construction, material, service and location were also types of the future tabernacle that God would build. Indeed, much of the truth required today to properly build local churches is symbolically hidden in the pattern and structure of the tabernacle.

> *Now Moses was faithful in all His house as a servant, for a testimony of those things which were to be spoken later. (Hebrews 3:5)*

Because of his intimacy with God, David is called a man after God's own heart. The desires of his heart reflected what was also in the heart of God. When we read the Psalms, we find them filled with revelations on the house of God. The following are some examples:

> *One thing I have asked from the Lord, that I shall seek; that I may dwell in the house of the Lord all the days of my life, to* ***behold the beauty of the Lord, and to meditate in His temple.*** *(Psalm 27:4)*

O Lord, I love the habitation of Thy house, the ***place where Thy glory dwells.*** *(Psalm 26:8)*

Glorious things *are spoken of you, O City of God. (Psalm 87:3)*

How ***blessed*** *is the one whom You choose and* ***bring near to You to dwell in Your courts*** *. . . . (Psalm 65:4)*

Great is the Lord, and greatly to be praised, in the city of our God, *His holy mountain. Beautiful in elevation, the joy of the whole earth, is Mount Zion in the far north, the city of the great King.* ***God in her palaces has made Himself known as a stronghold.*** *(Psalm 48:1-3)*

How lovely are Your dwelling places, O Lord of hosts! — How blessed are those who dwell in Your house! ***They are ever praising You. How blessed is the man whose strength is in You; in whose heart are the highways to Zion.*** *(Psalm 84:1, 4-5)*

O Lord, ***who may abide in Your tent?*** *Who may dwell on Your holy hill?* ***He who walks with integrity, and works righteousness, and speaks truth in his heart.*** *(Psalm 15:1-5)*

For the Lord has chosen Zion; He has desired it for His habitation. ***This is My resting place forever;*** *here I will dwell, for I have desired it. (Psalm 132:13-14)*

Through the words of David, we discover many new truths concerning the house of God. For example:

- It is both a mountain and a city.
- It is a place of His glory.
- It is a place of worship and prayer.
- It is a place of great supply, abundance, joy, strength and defense from evil.
- It is to become the place of God's everlasting habitation, which He refers to as the place of His eternal rest.
- It is a place to behold the beauty of the Lord, to meditate, to be nourished and strengthened by an abundance of goodness and lovingkindness from His presence.

The Reality

What was pattern and shadow in the Old Testament began to take on reality when the Builder Himself, the Lord Jesus Christ, came to earth. He came as the precious, tested cornerstone firmly placed by His Father to be the foundation for our salvation, and thus, for the house of God (Isaiah 28:16).

He is the foundation for the house of God, the Son over His Father's house, the High Priest in the house and is the builder of the house (1 Corinthians 3:11; Hebrews 3:1-6).

The Greek word for "administration" in Ephesians 1:10 is OIKONOMIA which literally means "management of a house or household" (OIKOS, a house; NOMOS, a law). This verse of scripture clearly expresses the place of Jesus in His Father's house.

> *. . . in all wisdom and insight He made known to us the* ***mystery of His will,*** *according to His kind intention which He purposed in Him (Christ) with a view to "a management of (His) house" suitable to the fulness of times, that is,* ***the summing up of all things in Christ,*** *things in the heavens and things on earth . . . . (Ephesians 1:8-10)*

Jesus is the center focus of all things in the house of God!

> *For* ***from*** *Him and* ***through*** *Him and* ***to*** *Him are* ***all things.*** *To Him be the glory forever. Amen. (Romans 11:36)*

> *He is before all things, and in Him all things hold together . . . . that He Himself will come to have first place in everything. (Colossians 1:17-18)*

Jesus has promised to prepare a dwelling place for each child of God in His Father's house.

> *In My Father's house are many dwelling places; if it were not so, I would have told you; for I go to prepare a place for you. If I go and prepare a place for you, I will come again and receive you to Myself, that where I am, there you may be also. (John 14:2-3)*

Although we are saved by the mercy and grace of God, and not by works, our rewards will be based on our works while here on earth (1 Corinthians 3:10-14). It appears that the glory of our future dwelling place will depend upon the "spiritual material" that we send up from our life here below for the Lord to build with.

One cannot separate the glory of God from His house. God is not building a structure to contain Himself; He is building a place to fully express Himself, where the full glory of His presence and government will be visible to all creation. This is evident in the scriptures that describe the city He has built coming down to earth (Revelation 21:2-3, 9-11, 23).

When the tabernacle was completed by Moses, the glory of His presence filled the place. The same appearance of His glory occurred when Solomon's temple was completed. These incidents were but shadows of the full glory of His presence that will one day mark the place of His eternal rest, the city that He is building today.

That is where our hope and expectations are to lie.

> *For here we do not have a lasting city, but **we are seeking the city which is to come.** (Hebrews 13:14)*

It is in our relationship with and obedience to Christ that we can gain His glory (Romans 5:1-5).

> *. . . because God has chosen you from the beginning for salvation through sanctification by the Spirit and faith in the truth. It was for this He called you through our gospel **that you might gain the glory of our Lord Jesus Christ.** (2 Thessalonians 2:13-14)*

The glory of Christ is not simply a resplendent brilliance, it is a visible expression of those virtues that comprise His divine character; virtues that God Himself personally identified to Moses (Exodus 34:6-7). Those qualities of His being are: He is compassionate and gracious, slow to anger, full of mercy and truth; He forgives iniquity, transgression and sin, yet He is just.

These are the same qualities that Jesus exhibited in His life and ministry on earth (John 1:14-18; Hebrews 1:3).

We can gain His glory as we allow the Holy Spirit to transform us into His image. The choice is ours!

> *But we all, with unveiled face, beholding as in a mirror the glory of the Lord, are being transformed into the same image from glory to glory, just as from the Lord, the Spirit. (2 Corinthians 3:18)*

It is more than simply being saved and assured of going to heaven. There are rewards to be gained.

> *. . . for if we died with Him, we will also live with Him;* ***if we endure, we will also reign with Him.*** *(2 Timothy 2:11-12)*

Every believer is promised a future resurrection body that bears the image of Christ; this is part of our inheritance in Christ. However, our rewards will vary, glory for some and disappointment for others (2 Corinthians 5:10). Resurrection glory will vary!

> *There is one glory of the sun, and another glory of the moon, and another glory of the stars; for star differs from star in glory. So also is the resurrection of the dead . . . . (1 Corinthians 15:41-42)*

> *For we know that if the earthly tent which is our house is torn down, we have a building from God, a house not made with hands, eternal in the heavens. For indeed in this house we groan, longing to be clothed with our dwelling from heaven,* ***inasmuch as we, having put it on, will not be found naked.*** *(2 Corinthians 5:1-3)*

Before Adam fell into sin, he was apparently clothed in the glory of God. The story of salvation is the great work that God is doing in bringing many sons to glory through the sanctifying work of His Son, the Lord Jesus Christ (Hebrews 2:9-11). The hope of our reward in the resurrection is to be clothed with the glory of God.

Building for Glory

The issue that we all face is how to properly build our personal and corporate lives on the foundation that God has provided for us in His Son, the Lord Jesus. Paul expresses it this way:

> *. . . but* ***each man must be careful how he builds upon it.*** *For no man can lay a foundation other than the one which is laid, which is Jesus Christ. . . . If any man's work which he has built on it remains, he will receive a reward. (1 Corinthians 3:10, 11, 14)*

The question of how to build begins in finding our place in His body through a life-union with the Lord Jesus; a place where one can be fitted together with brothers and sisters and built together for a dwelling of God in the Spirit.

Jesus builds us together through ministries of relationships, spiritual gifts and the five-fold ministries which promote spiritual growth and develop godly character. The key word is always "edification." The word "edify" is translated from the Greek word OIKODOMEO which literally means "to build a house" (DEMEO, to build; OIKOS, a house). All ministry is to edify the church (1 Corinthians 14:12, 26; Ephesians 4:29).

In his first epistle, Peter describes believers as "living stones" who are built together to form the Lord's house (1 Peter 2:4). His emphasis is not a pile of stones, but of stones carefully selected and shaped to fit a specific place where they will be cemented to other stones according to the Builder's plan. The goal is not conformity (i.e. like bricks) but diversity where stones differ from one another in size, shape and appearance. This speaks of men and women who are unique in their gifting, grace and service being fitted and built together in a local expression of body life.

Body life is a functioning relationship in the Spirit; it is not simply a religious organization of believers assembled around a set of Bible creeds.

Paul describes the relationship that bonds believers together as "joints and ligaments" (Colossians 2:19; Ephesians 4:16). Joints and ligaments define the relational interfaces between members that enable them to work together in harmony; a vital part of the building process.

The bottom line in everything, whether it is body ministry, fellowship, worship, teaching, enduring afflictions, etc., is gaining the character qualities from which the glory of Christ emanates. We are not dead stones, we are living stones possessing free wills to cooperate with the Lord in the building process. Christ in us is our hope of glory! Only He can do the work, but we must humble ourselves and yield to Him.

God can only use broken men; those who have laid down human values of greatness to embrace the way of the Spirit. This transition requires the following personal commitments:

- Study and obey the word of God to distinguish and separate what is soulish from the spiritual (Hebrews 4:12).
- Discipline the use of the window of our natural senses; we must not be led or governed by our physical senses.
- Develop a sensitivity to and use of the window of our spiritual senses.

For all who are being led by the Spirit of God, these are sons of God. (Romans 8:14)

How does all this fit together in the purpose of God?

- The universal body of Christ is made up of the churches in all nations, which includes the nation of Israel (Romans 11:25-26).
- The church of a nation is made up of regional churches.
- A regional church is made up of local churches.
- A local church is made up of house churches.
- A house church is made up of families.
- A family is made up of individual believers.
- An individual believer is made up of body, soul and spirit—God's building blocks!

In conclusion, grace and mercy are extended to us to enter into the great stream of events that began back in eternity, events initiated by God which will one day consummate in the completion of His purpose, the dwelling place of God among men. I pray that my words will help the reader lay aside soulish things, and be conformed to the image of Christ; a living stone of glory in the house of God!

APPENDIX

The various models of body, soul and spirit, that have been presented in the text, are all based on easy to understand graphics that clearly distinguish between soul and spirit. The truths in chapters 1 and 2 are foundational to all subsequent models. These truths can be extended into many other graphic presentations to create a resource library for the school of ministry in local churchs. For example, Figures 14, 15 and 16 illustrate how the principles of ministry can be applied to teaching on the family. Figure 14 addresses pre-marriage counseling; Figure 15 concerns ministry between husband and wife in marriage, and Figure 16 addresses parental ministry to children.

Churches today are generally overseen by a pastor or senior pastor. This is different than the local churches of the first century, which were often a united fellowship of house churches, that were overseen by a collegial eldership. These elders were chosen by the apostles, not simply because of their spiritual giftings, but primarily because they possessed proven character qualities related to their personal, family, church and community lives (1 Timothy 3:1-7; Titus 1:5-8). They were men who were accountable to one another. Through their lives and ministry they sought to be examples to the saints, as well as to care for and to equip them (1 Peter 5:1-4; Acts 20:28). They were supported in their ministry by deacons who facilitated the service of elders by handling tasks related to issues such as supervision of food distribution or other delegated responsibilities (Acts 6:1-6). Their character qualifications were similar to those for elders (1 Timothy 3:8-13). The Old Testament pattern of elders and deacons is found in the service of Aaron and his sons (elders) and the service of the Levites (deacons) in their joint responsibility as priests in the tabernacle of Moses (Numbers 3:5-10, 17-39; 18:1-8). The tabernacle was a type of the church and Moses was a type of Christ.

Figure 17 illustrates the ministry of shepherding in a local church.

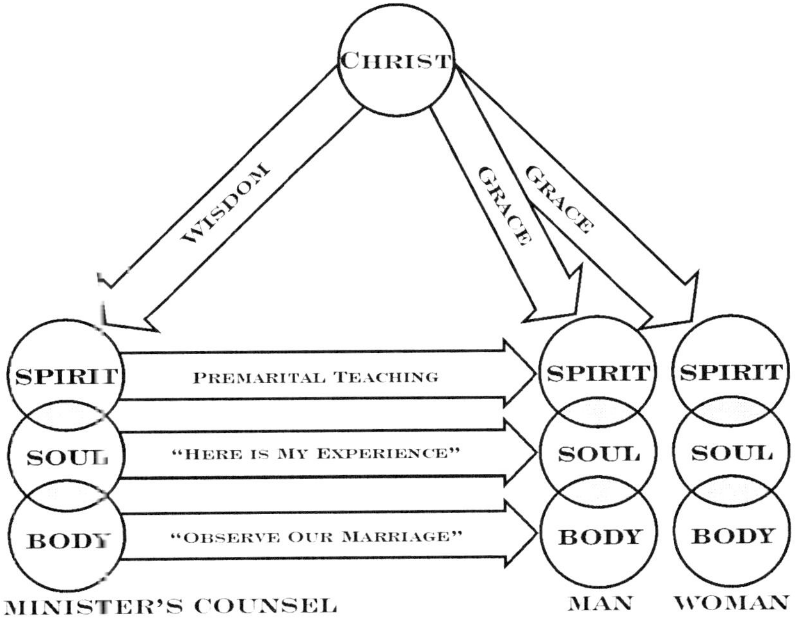

1. Covenant Union - Mal. 3:13-16; Mt. 19:4-9
2. Walking Out Covenant - Eph. 5:22-22; 1 Pet. 3:1-9
3. Headship & Responsibilites - 1 Cor. 11:3-12
4. Procreation - Ps. 127:3-5; 139:13-16; 1 Cor. 7:1-5
5. Ministry of Wife as Helpmate, She Completes Her Husband - Gen. 2:18
6. Honest Communications
7. Mutual Honor & Trust
8. Homemaking & Hospitality
9. Finances
10. Continuing Courtship

MINISTRY ON MARRIAGE

Figure 14

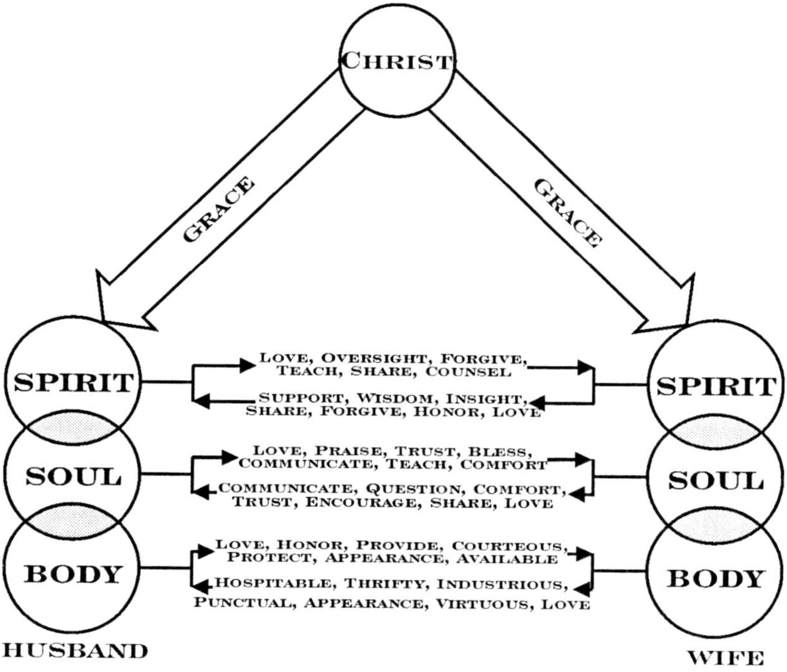

1. LIVING A COVENANT LIFE TOGETHER
2. MINISTERING GRACE TO ONE ANOTHER
3. PRACTICING FORGIVENESS
4. MAINTAINING TIMES OF FELLOWSHIP TOGETHER
5. AGREE ON PRIORITIES
6. PRAY TOGETHER DAILY
7. BE COMMITTED TO HOSPITALITY
8. ACCEPT WHAT CAN'T BE CHANGED

MINISTRY IN MARRIAGE

FIGURE 15

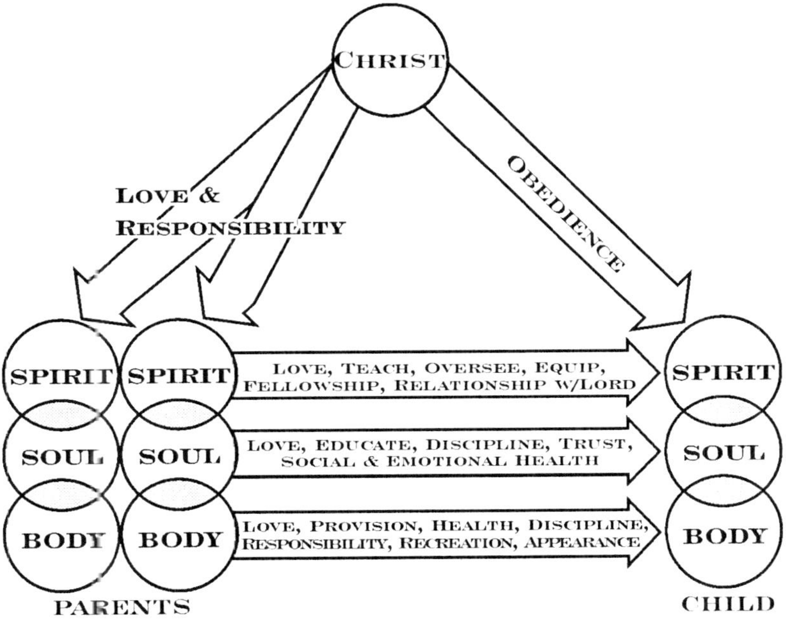

- Speak with One voice
- Train by Instruction & Example
- Parenting Requires Time
- Define Clear Boundaries, Good Habits
- Avoid Permissiveness & Over-Protection
- Discipline in Love (Pr. 23:12-14; 29:15, 17)
- Establish Courtesy, Honor, Respect
- Children Must Know the Lord
  - Must Know They are Loved
  - Endorsement of Worth
  - Have Peer Fellowship

MINISTRY TO CHILDREN

FIGURE 16

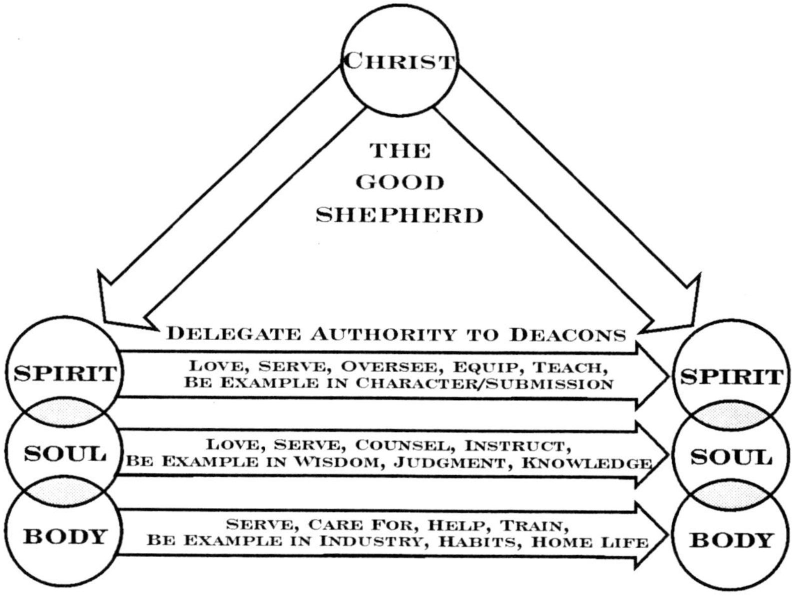

- ACTS 14:23; 20:17-35; 1 PET. 5:1-4; HEB. 13:7, 17
- QUALIFICATIONS: 1 TIM. 3:1-7; TIT. 1:5-8
- COMMITMENT: MT. 20:25-28; 2 TIM. 2:24-26: JN. 21:15-17
- INSTRUCT BY WORD AND EXAMPLE HOW THE SHEEP ARE TO HEAR AND OBEY THE VOICE OF THE LORD
- BE ACCOUNTABLE TO ONE ANOTHER
- MAINTAIN THE CENTRALITY OF CHRIST

SHEPHERDING

FIGURE 17

To purchase additional copies of:

BODY, SOUL SPIRIT

GOD'S BUILDING BLOCKS

please contact:

Selah Publishing Group, LLC

Toll free 800-917-2665

or visit our website at

www.selahbooks.com

Printed in the United States
1114300003BA

9 781589 300866